Witchcraft

This book includes:

Wicca Beginner's Guide

Wicca Book of Shadows

Wicca Herbal Magic

Wicca Candle Magic

Wicca Altar

Valerie W. Holt

Contents

Wicca

Beginner's Guide

A Beginner's Guide to Mastering Wiccan Beliefs, Rituals, and Magic

Valerie W. Holt

Introduction

Wicca is the religion that is most closely associated with paganism. However, it is merely one branch of paganism, one out of the hundreds that exist. There are a lot of rumors and misnomers about the Wiccan religion, and what it is associated with. One of these common misnomers is that it is correlated with Satanism. This is incorrect, along with many other rumors.

We'll be addressing those throughout this book. This is a five book series that is geared towards educating and encouraging young spirituals in their journey to become the best version of themselves in this religion.

Section 1

What is Wicca

The Religion

Started in the early twentieth century, Wicca is a contemporary pagan religion that revolves around the use of spiritual and physical energy that manifests itself in and around us. While there are so many different takes on this religion, they are all based on the same fundamentals, to keep the peace, and stay as one with the earth.

This religion is one that does not contain a central authority. This means that there are not really any churches that you have to attend, and every partaker is responsible for their own soul. You have to find yourself in the religion, rather than go to an establishment of worship and listen to someone drone on and on about the boring particulars; you have to follow them yourself. This also makes the Wiccan religion a lot easier to stick with, because it is always more interesting to discover things for yourself.

A lot of people consider the Wiccan religion to be the founding of paganism. However, it is quite the opposite. Paganism is the founding of the Wiccan religion. Wicca is based on ancient paganism ideals and contemporary spiritualism. There is a common theme among the Wiccan practices that is a little newer, and that is to becoming one with the earth. A lot of ancient paganism dealt with using the earth, rather than working with it.

The Wiccan religion is one that is filled with magic and wonder. However, it is often abused, and that is why it gets a bad reputation. If you are planning on following your spirit in the Wiccan ways, then be sure that you are prepared to handle the responsibility that comes with this religion. Otherwise, you should go about pretending that this religion doesn't exist.

Now, what exactly is Wicca? Up to this point, I have been beating around the bush just a tad. The truth is that it is hard to define Wicca, as there is so much that goes into it, and it is not the same for everyone. Everyone experiences Wicca a little differently, and that is what makes it so appealing.

If you had to define this religion, the best way to do so would be to describe it as a religion in where your main goal is to unlock the magic in your soul. Each person has a goal in this religion. And that goal boils down to wanting to find magic in life. While you may not get a whole "Harry Potter" level magic going on, you may find yourself being able to do some beginner "Eragon" magic. And even if you don't find the physical magic, you may find the spiritual magic that every person has locked away inside of them.

You do not have to worry if you don't achieve physical magic. Very few do, and there have not been many if any, accounts of drastic magic being done. That is not to say that it is not possible. The accounts may be locked inside the mind of someone who is locked away for being considered "crazy." You have to remember that neo-Christianity is not very accepting of other people's religions. This trend started back when Roman Catholicism took hold of the minds of many and swept through many countries. All other religions, including paganism religions, were deemed as heresy, and they were considered punishable by law. Thus, small accounts have stuck throughout the years. Since then, as Roman Catholicism has spread, and broken off into branches and Christianity.

The Known and Well Documented History

The history of this religion is actually not as old as people believe it to be. While it takes some old beliefs and adds it into the religion, it is actually a more contemporary form of paganism that is being celebrated along with other theologies to make it the best of all of them. Some older paganists call Wicca "picking and choosing" however, this is quite incorrect. Wicca is taking parts of all different religions, the parts that seem to coincide with each other and building from there.

In the early 1920's, the Wiccan culture began to emerge from the ashes of paganism. By this time, most of the world had turned to Christianity and had denounced any type of religion that was not a form of Catholicism or Christianity. Recall, that at this time, in many countries it was illegal to practice any religion that was not the main religion of your country, so that really made it hard for other religions to be documented.

The Wiccan religion started on the basis that the early witch hunts of England were in fact, based on the wrong ideas, and that the witches were followers of Satanism. This is known as a witch-cult theory, and it is a very popular theory that surrounds the witch trials of early England and Salem. First expressed by a German professor, Karl Ernst Jarcke, the idea quickly flared throughout the world as a very plausible thought, and people soon decided to build a religion that would show the world that true witches have nothing to do with Satanism.

Gerald Gardner became known as the father of Wicca around 1936. He decided that the Wiccan beliefs should become a true religion rather than just a bunch of people who share a similar belief. He also decided that there should be a few basic rules to the religion, rather than everyone making up their own, but all in all the rules were not that bad. Gardner founded a coven after purchasing a country club in his area and made it their headquarters. The coven ran almost entirely on money brought in by its members.

However, despite being the founding father of Wicca, his craft was more called Gardenerism, and was based more on the old religion than what Wicca is today. He also never referred to the craft as Wicca. However, he did once mention the group as being *The Wicca*, which is where the term Wicca originated from. Gardenerism was the prominent form of Wicca in the British Isles and England.

The British tabloids started to give Wicca a bad image. However, that seemed just to fuel the interest further (back then, no one believed the mainstream media). They knew since the tabloids were trying to bring it down, they felt threatened. That must have meant that there had to be something good associated with the religion. So people started getting more into it, and it spread throughout the country.

Around this time in history, a man named Alexander Sanders started to mold the Wicca religion, and add in more focus on ceremonial magic. This form of Wicca was known as Alexandrian Wicca. It is the most popular form of Wicca practiced today. This lays its focus on magic that is generally only used for good.

Gardenerism is focused on the belief that there are three levels of witches, a white witch (only does good), a gray witch (does bad things for good reasons), and a black witch (dark magic users, banned from most Wiccan cults). Gardenerism tried to show the difference between the three witches and publicly rebuked those who dabbled in dark magic.

Alexandrian Wicca rebukes all witches who use magic for anything other than pure good. That is why Wicca today is a nice balance between Alexandrian Wicca and Gardenerism, however, the balance is skewed more towards Alexandrian Wicca in the west.

By the 1990's, Wicca had become somewhat of a trend. This disgusted true Wiccans, because they were in it for life and didn't see it as a trend. It was their religion, not just something that they did for fun, but a lot of the younger generation seemed only to want to get into it for fun. This caused a lot of true Wiccans to start going back to the old ways to separate themselves from the trend following sheeple.

Unlike most religions, since this one is fairly new, it does not have a rich, well known history that spans thousands of years. It actually has a very brief well known history. However, there is also Wiccan history that is not as well known. However, because it is not documented, most of the unknown history is considered speculation.

Unknown History of Wicca

The first theory is that Wicca is directly tied to the Salem witch trials in the 1800's. The belief is that other pagan worshipers were so outraged that they decided they were going to show the world that witches were not to be toyed with. The thought was that they were going to wreak havoc on the world by invoking their powers in the name of themselves, and show the world that they had nothing to do with Satan, and the power came from them alone. However, a few people talked some sense into their covens and convinced them that violence would only make things worse. This is where Gardenerism comes from, with the White, Gray, and Black witches. It is rumored that if a coven discovered a black witch, they would bind them, and cure them of the darkness. This cure could kill the witch if they were too tied to the darkness. This is, of course, not well known, because the Wiccan culture tried its best to look like a clean cut society to keep the witch burnings at bay. Alexandrian Wicca decided that any magic that was not used purely was bad, and most accounts of even gray magic were wiped out.

Another theory is that voodoo queens in Louisiana, and the bayou area are Gray witch Wiccans who were banned from a coven. They were banned from their covens for using hexes, and thus they decided to become their own governesses and start their own culture of sorts. If you live near the French Quarter, or pretty much anywhere in Louisiana, you have probably heard of voodoo queens, and maybe you even know one. Once upon a time, an unnamed Louisiana slave who practiced the Wiccan religion and was part of a coven decided to hex her slave owner for taking her baby and selling him. The slave owner died of unknown causes, but the coven found traces of dark magic around the slave and pieced together the puzzle. The woman was set free, but she was no longer allowed to be a part of the coven. She found herself a little shack in the bayou, and so enthralled with the feeling that the dark curse gave her, she decided she would open up shop. She wanted to clear her conscience by helping people do bad things to people that hurt them. A few of her friends in the coven decided to join her, and thus began the tradition of Voodoo queens.

There is a theory out there that not only should Wiccans cast a circle with the four known elements, but there is a fifth element that is overlooked. This element is known as spirit. It is often invoked in Native American rituals, and in the early 2,000's, PC and Kristen Cast wrote a book series known as the House of Night. It is about vampires. However, these vampires are very close to the Wiccan religion. In fact, it is a mix of Wiccan religion and Native traditions with vampires thrown in. While the book series is entirely fictional, there are some great things in it that can help you learn more about the Wiccan traditions.

Alexander Sanders was rumored to adapt the Wiccan traditions to the Native American rituals. That is why the two are so strikingly similar. In fact, smudging and a lot of spells are extremely similar, or even interchangeable. It is said that Sanders and some of his friends came across a Native American chief who taught them about the rituals. However, it is not just any Native ritual; it is the rituals of the Cherokee Natives that Wicca resembles.

That is really all that is out there in the unknown history that is even slightly validated. There are a lot of other claims that are extremely outrageous, and though they might be true, this book is for instruction, not fiction.

Section 2

Wiccan Beliefs

Unlike Christianity, which celebrates monotheism, meaning they only worship one god, Wicca is dualistic. Meaning, Wiccans worship not one but two gods. This is based on the gender separation of gods and goddesses, and the belief that we are created from a torrid love affair from these deities. This is also common with Hinduism and Taoism. If you do not know what Taoism is, think Yin and Yang. It is the religion that believes that the Yin and Yang represent the sun god and the moon goddess.

The Wicca religion celebrates two deities as well, the Horned God, and the Triple Goddess. These deities are seen as two lovers who have the responsibility of making sure that their followers keep themselves in line, and do good for the world. They are actually not that invasive in their subjects lives, however, they are often the ones that are called upon to help you complete your spells.

However, not all Wiccans are dualistic. Some are polytheistic. This means that they believe that there are a lot of deities out there that make it possible for them to access all of the spells that they do. These Wiccans operate under the belief that it is too much responsibility for even one god to control everything in an area, so there are many lesser deities that handle the more minor responsibilities and the minor spells. This is a very valid belief, and if you feel that it suits you, then feel free to believe that way. This book will include all of the major deities in the religion.

Dualism

Dualism is the belief that there are two deities in a religion. This belief is portrayed in many religions and is based on the belief that having two opposite deities keeps a balance of good and evil, and that we are created from this balance, which is why there are always good and bad people. Everyone has a bit of good and evil within them; it just depends on which they choose to follow.

The Goddess

Also known as Mother Goddess, she is the one you call on for love and healing spells. Spells to do with nature are also under her calling. She is known as a Triple Goddess, as she is seen as the Virgin. The Mother, and the Crone. She is in control of moon rotations, and the growth of the earth. It is said that she graced Mother Theresa, and created the tide in the oceans. She is the Goddess of fertility and love as well.

The Mother Goddess is generally called upon by women, as she influences her gender the most. However, it is not uncommon for a male to call upon her as well, as love is a powerful thing, and even men want it too.

There is not much that is known about the Goddess because as stated previously, the deities pretty much keep to themselves. There are no ten commandments that you have to follow. You don't have to pray every day. There is no set book of rules and regulations that you have to follow. There is no threat of dying and spending your eternity in a fiery pit of torture if you do not believe.

The Horned God
This is where people confuse Wicca for Satanism. We worship a horned god. However, he is the sun god and has nothing to do with Satan. The horns are because he is in control of animals and the animalistic side of nature, and has the horns of a bull. He is the caretaker of males and the overseer of protection. Protection spells are mainly done through him. Light spells are as well. The Horned God is also linked to the Greek God Pan, the animal god that disappeared without a trace and has since been obscured by history. It is said that he still exists in a different realm, and has since decided to govern the Wiccans. He is the symbol of virility in males and is often portrayed with multiple interpretations.

Again, there is not a lot on the Horned God, without crossing into different religions. He is pretty hands off as well. This is why a lot of Wiccans believe that there are more deities in this religion, because the more deities there are, the less they mingle with humans to avoid confusing them.

Polytheism

Polytheism is the belief that there are many deities that control the earth in the religion. This is based on the belief that the more deities there are, the fewer hands on the deities become so that they do not relay the wrong information. They control certain spells and do not cross into other territories. This is the only way that they interact with humans, and since this seems to be the case with the Wicca religion, many people follow the polytheism belief rather than the dualistic ideals.

On top of the Horned God and the Triple Goddess, there are a few other deities. Not many, and some of them are small group deities, so, unfortunately, there is not enough information about them to include them. Let's, however, discuss the main two. These two are very different from each other as well.

Dryghten

The star goddess is complimented with creating the cosmos, and she is the one you speak to when you wish upon a star. She is very vengeful against the human race because Mother Goddess decided that she should have no human contact with them. She tried to sleep with the humans, which Mother Goddess considered would produce volatile offspring. And that is the why wishes are often not granted. She does, however, have a few weak spots and will grant a wish to someone who has won her heart.

Many Wiccans have gained her heart by worshiping her as a real deity. This softens her up, and she will help with spells that are farfetched from working. Such as finding someone you bumped into three years ago on a subway and can't stop thinking about, despite the fact that you never got a name.

The One

Also known as *the All,* this deity is considered to be the controlling deity, and above all other gods and goddesses of the religion. He is considered to be all-powerful, and omniscient, and sometimes referred to as he or she, as there is no defining gender to this deity. Think of this deity similar to that of the Christian faith.

Little is known about the One, but what we do know is that he controls what the other gods do and ensures that they are doing it correctly. He has little to no contact with humans and mainly deals with the Horned God and Mother Goddess.

Everyone Else

Those are the main deities in the Wiccan religion, however, if you decide to join a coven, then there may be a few more deities that you will learn about. These are the fundamental ones that any coven that is polytheistic knows about, the rest are coven specific, and with all the covens out there, we would be here all day with just coven specific deity information. Plus, since some deities are only believed involved in single covens, there is not enough information out there to really include them at all.

Ritual Beliefs

There are many other parts of the Wiccan beliefs that do not include the gods and goddesses. These beliefs pertain to celebrations and other rituals that are said to be important. These should all be taken into account and acted upon because they are the core of the Wiccan traditions.

The Wheel of the Year

This is one of the biggest Wiccan rituals out there. The Wheel of the year is not one single celebration. It is a collection of eight celebrations throughout the year. Each celebration is cause for excitement and magic because during these celebrations it is believed that the gates between the magic and mortal worlds are open more so than they are throughout the rest of the year.

Some covens only celebrate four to six of the eight celebrations. We call them party poopers. Just kidding, they believe that the other two are weaker veiled celebrations that invite in the dark magic rather than the good, white magic, so they stay away from them.

The wheel of the year follows the solstices as well. The solstices are important because it's when the magic is most charged through the air, and this is when the witches get the most power from the world. If you miss out on the solstices celebrations, you will miss out on a big chance to do some great magic. This is problematic because you want to do the best that you can if you're serious about Wicca, and if you miss out on the best time to charge your crystals, then you may miss out on your true potential. However, we are getting a little off track. The celebrations in the Wheel of the Year are called Sabbats.

Sabbats

Sabbats are the celebrations throughout the year that Wiccans celebrate. These are important celebrations that are considered sacred and should be treated as such. This means that you should treat them with the utmost respect, rather than make it a commercialized event as some religions have done with their holidays.

The eight Sabbats are all due to the solstices and equinoxes, but one is not. They will start at the beginning of the year, and continue to the end of the year, as per when they are celebrated in the Northern Hemisphere.

- **Candlemas:** This is the celebration of the first true signs of spring. It is generally celebrated on the first or the second of February in the northern hemisphere and on the first of August in the southern hemisphere. This celebration is to praise the Mother Goddess and ask her to bring forth the spring to rid them of the cold and bring forth the flowers and bees to start the pollination process of the garden cycle.

- **Ostara:** This is the celebration of the spring, or vernal, equinox. This is generally celebrated on the twenty-second of March in the northern hemisphere, and the twenty-second of September in the southern hemisphere. This celebration is to ask the Mother Goddess to restore fertility to the animals, and to the women. This celebration is for the celebration of life, and bringing forth what was dead, and bringing it back to life.

- **Beltane:** Celebrated on the first of May in the northern hemisphere, and the first of November in the southern hemisphere, it is the celebration of the full flowering of spring. It is during this time, that the Wiccans prepare to lay out their gardens, and are wishing for prosperity from the Mother Goddess. This is the time where it is most important to please the Goddess, as you want to be bountiful, and if you have offended her, she may avenge her honor on your harvest.

- **Litha:** In the northern hemisphere this is celebrated on the twenty-first of June, and on the twenty-first of December in the southern. This is the summer solstice, and it is the celebration of hard work. During this celebration, you ask the horned god to give you the strength to do your duties throughout the summer, and (males) ask him for virility throughout the year.

- **Lammas:** No this has nothing to do with a furry, spitting, horse-like animal. It has to do with the first fruits of the year. Celebrated on the first of August up north, and the first of February down south, it is when you thank the Mother Goddess for giving you a successful crop that year, and if you have properly thanked her, she may give you an even better harvest.

- **Modron:** Celebrated on the twenty-first of September in the north, and the twenty-first of March in the south, this is the celebration of the autumnal equinox. This is when you harvest your crops and thank the Mother Goddess and the Horned God for their help in your prosperity. It is during this time that you take a portion of your crop and burn an offering for the Gods who helped you.

- **Samhain:** This is also known as Halloween, and is celebrated on the thirty-first of October in the north and the thirtieth of April in the south. This is the celebration of the veil between life and death. It is also when the veil is at its flimsiest. Many Wiccans take advantage of this to speak with dead loved ones. However, some are known to do so irresponsibly which can cause problems.

☐ **Yuletide:** This is the winter solstice celebration where you are thankful for the year as it draws to a close and celebrates the rebirth of the sun. This celebration is for the Horned God. It is celebrated on the twenty-second of December north and twenty-first of June south.

These are the eight Sabbats, and as you can probably see, the only one that doesn't have to do with the turn of the seasons is Samhain. Samhain is also known as the most dangerous of all of the rituals. Some covens do not celebrate it, for fear the power may corrupt its members. However, to truly unlock your Wiccan power, it is best to celebrate all of the Sabbats rather than just the turn of the season ones. Make sure that you cast a circle, and close the circle when you are thanking the Gods, or talking with the dead. This is essential because you can cause some serious issues when you do not cast a circle, because then anyone can answer your call, including a demon. This is generally how most Wiccans get pulled into black magic. They didn't cast a circle when doing a spell or celebration, and a demon answered, enslaving the person to their will.

Esbats

Some spells and rituals have to be done during a cycle of the moon. These cycles are called esbats. If you do not make sure that you do the spell during the right esbat, then you will either get faulty results or no results. Don't be impatient, because that is how bad things start to unravel.

Esbats also have to do with when the tide comes in, and fertility cycles. You want to follow these well, so you know when the moon waxes and wanes. These things will have an effect on your spells, so keep that in mind.

The Elements

This is an important part of the Wiccan religion. The elements are there to use when you cast a circle, and each element is to be well respected. Some Wiccans only use the four elements. However, there are actually five. These elements are what give us life, and sustain us as we take each breath. These elements are the wind beneath us, the ground we walk on, the heat that keeps us warm, the water we drink, the spirit inside of us.

You always call the elements in a circle starting north. Then you move clockwise to each other element before moving into the center and calling your final element. Once you have cast your circle, the elements will create a circle of protection around you, and you will be able to cast your spell. It is imperative that you do not leave your circle.

Air

Air is the first element that you should call to your circle while you are facing north. This element is the wind that moves around you, and it is what you breathe.

To call this element, use this chant

You fill our lungs

caress our hair

violent yet gentle

I welcome you air

If you have a different summoning chant for air, feel free to use it. This is just the one that I have found to work best.

Fire

After summoning air, turn to the right, and summon fire. This is the element that gives us heat, and what we use to make our food to eat. This is an important element to the circle just like any other.

When you are summoning fire, use this chant.

Our hearths are warm

as we are with desire

you sustain our lives

I welcome you fire!

Again, if you have a different chant, feel free to use it.

Water

Water is an important element as well. It is what we drink, and it is what makes up most of our body. This is the element that we rely on the most to sustain us, and give us life. It is to the south, opposite of air, because they are equally balanced.

To summon the water element, use this chant

You fill the bodies

of your sons and daughters

keeping us whole

I welcome you water!

This is a good chant, but if you have a better one, you know the drill.

Earth

Balancing out fire, this is the element that you feel beneath your feet. This is what we are born from, and what our bodies will return to when we die.

To summon Earth, use this chant

We are born from you

and return to your dirt

You are our foundation

I welcome you Earth!

By know you probably know that if you have a better chant, to use it.

Spirit

The fifth and final element. This is the element that gives us the will to do things. It is our literal beings because it is what we are reduced to when we die. To call this element, and thus complete your circle, step into the center and cast your last element with this chant

You give us will

we never want to lose it

All we have when we die

I welcome you spirit!

I have tried several different chants, and this seems to be the only one that works for me. If you do happen to find a different one, definitely use it, because it may give you a stronger bond with the element.

Those are the elements that you have to work with. They are important, and they protect and serve you. Be sure to thank each one of them as you close your circle.

Other Beliefs of This Religion

Aside from the main beliefs that everyone seems to know about, there are smaller, lesser known beliefs that are a part of the Wiccan religion as well. Not every coven follows these, but a large majority do.

Reincarnation

This is one of the most controversial beliefs of the Wiccan religion. There is a belief that once you die, you are reborn into a new body. This belief itself is not really disputed; it is how you are reincarnated that is what causes the disputes. There many ideas surrounding this belief that it literally splits covens, and causes people to fly solo.

One of the beliefs is that if you lived a good life, then once you die, that is it—it is over. You don't have to redo it, and you no longer have to suffer. Some say if you are not reincarnated, once you die, that is it. Others say that once you die if you are not being reincarnated, you get to go to the Isle of Souls. This sounds ominous, and it hasn't been called this for a long time, but it is basically a heaven for your spirit. There is no pain, there is no suffering, and you are content to spend eternity there.

Another belief is that if you lived a good life, you get reincarnated, rather than the souls that were not as pure as yours. This is highly disputed because a lot of people say that if you die when you were good, then why should you be punished to live this life over again.

There is yet another belief that is everyone is reincarnated, just at different times, and no one directly dies. This belief involves limbo. Limbo is where your soul goes while it awaits reincarnation. A lot of religions refer to Limbo as a bridge between life and eternal death. If you are in limbo, it is said that you did not live a pure enough life to be immediately reincarnated, but you also did not live a bad enough life to be sentenced to eternal death. However, while in limbo, if you break the rules, you stand to be sentenced to eternal death. However, if you stay good while awaiting your time to be reincarnated, you will enter the world once more.

Many reincarnated spirits do not know that they are reincarnated, except when they are young, they may have some flashbacks from their previous lives. This is why little kids sometimes know things out of nowhere. In Wiccan beliefs, there is no other explanation for them knowing other than reincarnation.

Afterlife
Many Wiccans do believe that there is an afterlife. This is where you spend your time when you have died, and you do not need to be reincarnated. The Wiccan afterlife is not described like Christian afterlife. There is no paradise per se. And there are no streets of gold. It is a place for your spirit goes to rest, and relax for all eternity. Also, you can choose to be reincarnated if you find the rest phase too boring.

No other religion has the belief that after you move on to the "heaven" stage, you can move back to life. However, the Wiccan belief is that energy never stops moving, and since your spirit is pure energy, it makes sense that it would not want to stay complacent for all eternity.

Animism

Animism is the belief that everything has a spirit. That everything is living, even if it is an inanimate object. This applies the most to plants, the earth, and the elements. This belief is that you must respect all things because they feel just as we do.

This is based on the belief that you should always respect the earth. This includes the trees, and the grass, and plants. Many Wiccans believe that if you touch a tree, and summon Earth, you can feel the tree's feelings as if were your own.

The earth as an element really does feel. That is why Mother Goddess is often also called Mother Earth. To experience this feeling, go out to an area with a clearing, and lay down. Try to get as much of your skin touching the earth as possible by taking off your shoes and socks, and if it is warm enough wear a tank top. Let your hair fan out around you if it is long, removing it from the back of your neck. Lay as flat as you possibly can, and focus on slowing your breathing till it is at the rate of a sleeping person. Call earth to you. However, instead of using and invoking chant, use what I call a companion chant. This asks the element to come and join you, to assist you and allows the element to refuse to assist.

Earth I call you

In hopes that you will come

Help me see the pain you hold

show me the damage that was done.

By showing the earth that you care, it will most likely answer your call. If you are having trouble getting Earth to come to you, try focusing on your breathing. You may not be breathing slow enough. If you are too excited, it will not work, because Earth is a very sensitive element and is not a fan of extreme excitements.

You can try to feel if the water feels as well. However, you do not want too much of your body in the water, as drowning is a real danger.

To feel the water, go to a beach or a river bank, and stick your legs in. Stay sitting up or leaning back away from the water, and close your eyes. Listen to the sound of the waves, and make your breath match the rhythm of the water. Once you have the pattern of breathing down, call to water.

Water I call you

I ask you to join me

show me the problems

show me all I need to see.

After a couple of tries, you should be able to sense the emotions coming from the water. Water is not a shy element and will generally come if asked nicely.

Air and fire are harder to feel as one is almost intangible and the other will burn you. However, if you find a way to summon them and feel their emotions then you definitely should try.

Other Occult Systems

Wiccans are not against other occult systems, as some of them are good as well. However, they are wary of others, because too many of them front as a good group, but in reality, they are dabbling in black magic, or are entirely misinformed.

However, since Wicca was formed from other occult systems, they do not have any ill will with them, in fact, some covens learn new magic from other pagan occults. This is often encouraged to establish an open bond, but also to make sure that other groups are not dabbling in the dark arts of magic.

Remember that not all covens follow all of these beliefs, but a majority of them do.

Section 3

Witchcraft

Witchcraft

Witchcraft is the art of using magic to help you in everyday life. These spells can range from healing potions to curses that cause death. Witchcraft is a very varied subject, and it is looked upon as evil. People often portray witches as green evil beings that fly on broomsticks. Not all witches are bad. In fact, Wiccan witches are very helpful and want to heal the earth along with other people. Witchcraft itself is divided into three different parts.

Magic and Science

Witchcraft is often portrayed as mumbo jumbo. A lot of magic is based on science. For example, the property that different herbs have, along with the cycles of the moon. Though you can make up your own spells, you still have to know the basics of science. If you are making a potion, it is just like chemistry. In fact, a lot of the time it is chemistry, just taken to a magical level.

If you look at a lot of spells, you will find that there is a certain air of certainty to them. That is because they are based on the scientific knowledge of each herb that is included in them. When you are going to do a spell, just like with an experiment, you have to be precise. Otherwise, things could go very wrong. They could literally or figuratively blow up in your face.

Don't get scared, if you do it right, you could have a great outcome. Because just like in science, if you follow the directions, then you will find out that things go a lot smoother.

Of course, true scientists know that it is no fun if you can't find your own solutions to a problem. In our case, that's where making your own spells come in.

To get started you to know about:

☐ **Book of Shadows:** This is where you will write down all of your spells and potions, and you should definitely keep it safe because it is believed that if another witch gets a hold of your book of shadows, they can control you.

☐ **Herbs:** You have to choose the right herbs for your spell, based on the properties each herb has. For example, if you wanted to heal someone or something, a good herb to have is white sage based on its healing properties, and ability to soothe. Having the right herbs is essential because even if you have a good spell if you do not have the right herbs, you could end up with a disastrous result. Make sure that you get the right type of the herb that you need as well. Take sage, for example, there are many different types of it, and each one has different properties. If you used a purple sage, then you would not heal so much because it's known to cause drowsiness.

- **Moon Cycles:** You also need to know what each part of the moon cycle is related to. Not all spells are done on a full moon. And not all spells are done during a new moon. Some are at a certain point of the waning and waxing stages. You have to be sure to keep track of the moon cycles at all times if you are planning to do moon spells. However, most spells need at least one part of the moon cycle.

Once you acquainted with these concepts, then you can move on to actually creating spells. This is the most crucial point, because your chant has to make sense, and has to have a rhythm. It does not have to rhyme, but it does have to flow nicely. A poetry class doesn't hurt and will help write what you want to say with a good flow and make it sound like a song to please the gods.

Take this chant for example.

It is a spell to bless the year to come.

Mother Goddess

Father Sun

I ask you this year

to undo the hurt that has been done

and to look over those

who need a good hand

give me the ability

to help where I can.

Mother Goddess

Father Sun

I call to you like you are one

I ask your efforts

in my year to come

keep me bountiful

and my year fun.

After the chant, sprinkle turquoise dust on the ground, and a drop of wine. This spell must be done during the first full moon, at the beginning of the year, for it to work. You have to be calm and collected when you do it. You say the prayer over a crystal bowl filled with aloe, angelica, basil, bay, and chickweed. There are many other herbs that you could add into this spell to make it more powerful, but I just use it mainly as a protection spell.

I created this spell myself and have found that it genuinely works. Of course, there are still some bad times in life, but that is life, and you can't always prevent bad things from happening. This is mainly a spell of protection to avoid injuries and to heal the pain from the year before, and it really works. It is also a good blessing for heading into new friendships.

Ritual and Spell Work

The rituals are important because they are part of the religion and are what makes it unique. It's especially the spell work that you do that will make you unique. See, the fact of the matter is, every witch leaves a magical fingerprint after they do a spell. Meaning, no one else can ever replicate the spell quite like you. No one flourishes the wand or athame like you, no one pronounces every word just like you, and no one moves through the motions as you do. No two people do a spell exactly the same.

Rituals are how you do the spell and must be done before you start the spell. Rituals are like traditions. Sometimes it is best just to do them and leave them alone because they are identifiers of a group. One of the rituals is a circle. However, the circle is not what identifies Wiccans. It is how they open the circle. They go clockwise, rather than counter-clockwise as most paganist groups do. Also, most groups use candles to indicate a circle. Wiccans do not have to, but they can choose to if they so, please.

There are other rituals, such as what you need at your altar when performing a spell, and things of that nature as well. Wiccan altars are a leveled platform used for prayer and worship. Traditionally Wiccan altars have multiple symbolic items that worship the God and Goddess. They're used for casting spells, chants, and prayer. You as a Wiccan practitioner can personalize your altar as you wish.

The Wiccan religion is based on personal interpretation, so there are not too many rituals for spells. However, for celebrations, there are a lot of rituals. Such as making sure you use this time to charge your crystals (crystals are a large topic, which can be saved for a future book).

Spell work is more personal. It is how you do your spell, what you wear, how you stand, what spell you use. What your altar looks like, how you choose to mark your circle. All of those things are specific to you. You have to find your style and be consistent.

Spell work is also what makes you identifiable to other Wiccans, and covens. Covens, by the way, are territorial. An elder can sniff out any magic done in their territory, and often they will just ask you to go someplace else, but if you have stumbled upon dark Wiccans, it's not pleasant. Always talk to the earth before choosing a ritual area.

Tools

There are several tools that you need as a witch. These tools are essential and will help you in your craft. Beware, though, some of them may be beautiful, but when you have to use them, are not so pleasant.

The tools are as follows:

- **Athame:** A ceremonial knife that is used when you have to make a blood offering. This blade is to be decorative and kept sharp so that it pleases the Goddess while causing minimal pain and scarring upon use. When you use it, either prick the tip of your index finger or cut across the meaty part of your palm under your thumb - depending on the amount of blood needed. Often, you just have to cut the air with an athame.

- **Chalice:** The ceremonial cup that you often have to fill with wine as an offering to the earth. Sometimes you have to drink some of the wine as well, so if you are underage, it is best not to attempt those spells just yet. What has been done in the past is finding a red grape juice, as a substitute. Wouldn't want you to get in trouble for trying to heal the earth!

- **Wand:** Unlike in Harry Potter, often times, wands are just decorative pieces for your altar to please the goddess. The wand may need to be waved, but you do not have to have it for your power. The power comes from inside of you.

- **Pentacle:** This is different than a pentagram. It is a pendant with the five-point star encased in a circle on it. You use it to capture the energy of your spell and release it in a gentle and controlled manner. It sits on your altar at the front, so it can catch the energy before it is released dangerously.

There are other tools that you will often need as well, such as incense, smudge sticks, and candles, but you do not need those for a lot of rituals, so they are not essential tools.

Section 4

Your Wicca Quest

Read and Reach Out

The best way to begin your practices in this religion is to learn more about it. This means that you are going to have to read more sources than just this book alone. This book series will have a lot of information. However, learning never stops. Read and learn as much as you possibly can.

Reach out to other Wiccans for help. There are many out there that will be happy to mentor you and help you on your journey to becoming a great witch. Even if you do not want to join a coven, you can still ask for help from another loan wolf Wiccan. There are a lot of helpful forums online to help you find people and reach out. Reach out to these groups, and you'll get so much help—it is amazing. If you have a question, there is bound to be someone who has the answer.

Reaching out, and reading up are great ways to strengthen your belief and the magic in you. That is the goal of this religion, to strengthen the spirit and your belief in the religion.

Finding Where You Fit

Everyone wants to fit in, that is no secret. You want to feel like you are a part of something special, and it is the same with this religion. Just as there are several different sanctions of Catholicism and Christianity, there are many different branches of Wicca as well. In fact, it seems that the Wiccan religion is more flexible than even Christianity because Wiccans can make their own groups based on their belief system. Find your Wiccan community, and if you don't feel like you fit in, just go on your own way, and be a lone wolf. There are a lot of lone wolf Wiccans.

Covens

This is one of the best known types of Wiccan groups. Think of it as the country club for Wiccans. This is a large group of Wiccans that schedule regular meetings, and they often have club dues. Along with having dues, they often have a lot of rules and regulations that you don't see in a less strict group of Wiccans. This is because they want their coven to stay on the straight and narrow, and when you have too many witches in one group, then you could have some serious issues if one of them go, rogue. You as a part of the coven could get taken down with the rogue. So covens have to be kind of strict to keep things organized.

Covens are also great for beginners because there are rules. It may feel confining not to be able to find your style in the beginning, but you could grow to appreciate having so much help as you are learning. With covens, it is an all hands on deck deal. If one member is not up to par, then the members of the coven pitch in to help the weak link member. However, within a reasonable amount of time, there are possibilities you may get kicked out if you are in a pretentious coven. It is for the best if you are kicked out of a coven like that. A coven based on pretenses is one that has the most risk of turning to dark magic.

If you feel like a coven could be a good fit for you, you can go online to find one that is near you. There are a lot of online forums for Wiccan covens. This is often how they find new members in their area. If you are interested in it, try it for yourself.

Circles

A circle is a little different than a coven. The main difference is the size. A circle is always five people no matter what. One person for each element. The best part about this is, you can build your own circle pretty easily if you know four other Wiccans. Circles have rules and regulations like a coven, but they are often less strict because they do not have the sheer volume that covens have.

Circles are a great way to establish rituals and learning how to cast spells. If you do not feel like starting your own circle, you can look to see if there is a circle that is needing a new member online. Circles are great because you have people who can help you get to their level, and you don't have to worry about pretentiousness. You also don't have to worry about information overload, because there are a lot fewer people who are helping you.

When you are a part of a circle, it can be a great bonding experience as well. Since you don't have to pay dues to be in a circle, you find yourself making true bonds with the people you are working with. In a coven you are making forced bonds because you paid your money to be there, and you have to drag your butt there at least once a month. More if there is a celebration that month.

With a circle, you don't have to meet a certain amount of times if you choose not to. Most circles only meet when there is a need, or they feel they need to practice a spell. Needs could be a pollution problem in the area and needing to cast a protection spell on the trees and the earth. Or it could be a drought, and you need to beg to Mother Goddess to please bring rain. These are some of the needs that circles meet for. If one of you finds a spell that you think is useful, you may meet several days in a row to practice it until you have it down.

Circles also meet for celebrations. But rather than a whole ordeal where an Elder gets up and speaks about how you should thank the great goddess and horned god that you can gather with your brothers and sisters in this time of power and all the other things that Elders drone on about, you can actually be out there using your power. This is one of the best perks of being a part of a circle.

If you feel like you might fit in with a circle, you can either start your own or look for one in your area looking for a new member. You never know, you might find the place that you belong.

Eclectic

This is a group of Wiccans who really don't have a lot of rules, and are all at multiple different levels. It is great if you do not want to be pressured into having to become great in a short period of time, but the lack of rules and structure can cause a lot of rogues if you are not careful.

Eclectic groups are made up of a lot of different Wiccans, of all different ages. This makes it the most different from covens and circles because with circles, it is generally people around the same age, and with covens, there are groups of ages. And by a certain age, you are expected to be at a certain level. With an eclectic group, you may find a twenty-one-year-old at a level seven, and a forty-year-old at a level two. There is no limit for what level you have to be at what age. You just have to be willing to put in the time, and the effort to become the best you can be.

Eclectic groups are also a little out there when it comes to beliefs. They are like the hippies of the Wiccan world. They have some radical ideas that could change the world, but they are often looked down upon by "civilized" groups such as covens or circles. Because eclectic groups are so different, there is not a lot of information on what they do, but if you want to find out what they do, you could look online for an eclectic forum and learn more about if there is a group in your area taking members.

Solitary

Some Wiccans choose to learn the ropes by themselves, rather than let someone else take the reins. This is because they do not want to be steered in the wrong direction due to choosing the wrong group, or because they are just more comfortable being alone.

If you choose to be alone, you have to be good at self-motivating. However, it is a lot easier to learn at your own pace, and you don't have to search for a group.

Autumn Equinox Ritual

To get you started with your book of shadows (which I'll go into more detail, in my book *Wicca: Book of Shadows*) here is a ritual for an Autumn Equinox Celebration. It was taught to me by my great uncle who was also a Wiccan. You may find others, and you are free to choose the one you want, but here is the one that I know.

You will Need:

- The main tools for your altar

- Wine

- A fully charged crystal

- Crystal Bowl

- Crushed White Sage

- Crushed Basil

- Crushed Cayenne

- Crushed Cinnamon

Open your circle with your choice of gesture or candle. Greet all the elements with exuberance on this special night. This is the most important part because the elements want to feel your excitement at the change of the season.

Once you have opened your circle around your altar, take the charged crystal, and hold it over the bowl of crushed herbs. Try to hold it as still as possible at first.

While you are holding it still, chant this portion of the spell:

Hear my voice Gods, Goddesses, Elements

As this season starts to change

Leaves fall far from the trees

Things will never be the same

for who we are

is not who we were

be with me Goddess

as I choose to move forward

After you say forward, move the crystal in a circular motion clockwise above the bowl and finish the rest of the spell out.

Follow me, great God

as I turn over a new leaf

Follow me elements

as I strive for peace.

So it is said

so it shall be

I thank you all for joining me.

With that, you put the crystal around your neck, and take
the chalice full of wine and spill a drop on the ground. After
you spill the drop, thank the Horned God for joining you.
Drop another drop on the ground, and thank the Great
Goddess for being with you. Drop a third drop on the
ground, and thank the elements for joining you.

Finally, take a drink yourself and invite all three to become
a part of you. Once that is finished, you close your circle as
normal, making sure that you thank each element for its
part in your ceremony.

Wicca

Book of Shadows

A Book of Spells for Wiccans, Witches, and Other Masters of Magic

Valerie W. Holt

Previously

In my first book of this Wiccan series, we talked about the fundamentals of Wicca, the basics you need to know about beginning the religion, and finding out what kind of Wiccan you want to be.

In this book, you will learn more about spells. You will learn all sorts of spells that you can choose to keep in your own book of spells.

This is a book of spells—a Book of Shadows.

Before We Begin

Making a Book of Shadows

Finding the Right Book

Before you can start with making your book of shadows, you must first find the perfect book. While most book of shadows are created in leather, you can create yours out of anything you want. However, be warned, any fake substance such as the fuzzy bound books, will not hold your magic. Paper notebooks and spiral bounds do not do so well either. Leather bound books are found to be best. Go to your local office supply store, or buy one online.

Once you find the notebook section, you are going to have to get a little weird. You want a notebook that speaks to you so strong that you can feel a connection with it coursing through your veins. You do not want any old standard bound notebook. You want one that speaks to you. Whether you find one made of leather or organic paper materials, you want to feel the energy move within it. If you just pick one that doesn't mesh well with your energy, your spells won't be protected.

Once you have found a few potential notebooks, hold them to your chest and close your eyes. If you can imagine yourself writing for hours in the book, you have found the right one. If you cannot, keep looking. You want a strongly wielded spell book, not a book full of spells. That is a cookbook that only has recipes for disasters.

Why the Right Book is Crucial

There are bad witches out there. They want to use your spells and turn them into evil ones. If they get access to your spells, they can corrupt them. A spell book that meshes with your energy will not allow them to see it. An experienced witch can enchant their book to look blank to anyone who reads it but them. However, they can only do it if the book is loyal only to them.

You want a book that is loyal to you. Much like in the Harry Potter universe, where the wand chooses the wizard, in this case, the book chooses the witch. If you have a strong bond with your book of shadows, it will not be easy for someone to counteract the invisibility enchantment. The only way to counteract another witch's enchantment is to pour a drop of their blood on the book—or so it is told (I have never tried to steal another witch's book). Not many witches know that, though, and it may not even be true. It may just be an old wives' tale.

There is another rumor that talks about the real reason that a Wiccan should never let anyone near their book. It is said, that if someone gets a hold of another witch's book of shadows and gets past the enchantment, then that witch can control the true owner of the book. It becomes like a voodoo doll almost. You will be in the evildoer's clutches until you regain possession of your book. This may just be whispers in the dark, but you know what they say, fiction starts with a grain of truth—better safe than sorry.

How to Start Your Book

To start, a setup process is in order. You are going to need to cast a circle and have an altar set up. You want to cast a protection spell on your book, to keep it safe. Since you are just beginning you will not be strong enough for an invisibility spell, so you will just have to find a good hiding spot for your book of shadows.

To set up the altar and circle, you are going to need:

- your chosen book

- a charged crystal

- an athame

- a pentacle

- a smudge stick made up of

  - aspen

- beech

- blessed thistle

- fennel

- hyacinth

- pine

- walnut

- yarrow

⚹ a white candle

⚹ a yellow candle

⚹ a blue candle

⚹ a red candle

⚹ a green candle

⚹ a purple candle

⚹ a full moon

In *Wicca: Herbal* Magic, we will discuss how to make your own smudge sticks, but for now, if you can find a pagan store, you can ask them to make you one with these ingredients or you can order one online. If you wish to make your own, you can skip to *Wicca: Herbal Magic* to learn how to make your own and resume.

You may have noticed that you need a full moon. This is imperative, and it is best if you can do the spell at midnight. This will give you the most strength in a protection spell. You want the strongest protection that you can have for your book of shadows because you do not want anyone finding it.

When you get to your favorite spot, place the athame, charged crystal, and a pentacle on the altar around your smudge stick (place your stick in a fireproof bowl.) You should also have a white candle on your altar towards the back. This is imperative because you always want to light your smudge stick with a white candle.

Set up the candles in a circle around your altar according to their elements, setting the purple candle on the ground in front of the altar. (be careful not to kick it over). The circle should be big enough for you to move around your altar with ease and not worry about disturbing the candles. Light the white candle. As you welcome each element, light the corresponding candle. You have experience with casting a circle from the last book, I presume, so now it is just a matter of knowing which candle goes with which element.

Yellow = Air

Red = Fire

Green = Earth

Blue = Water

Purple = Spirit

After you have cast your circle, you want to be sure that you can move around without stepping out of the circle and halting the magic. Move candles if need be to expand the circle. Once all the candles are lit, and the white candle is back on the altar. It is time to invoke the goddess and horned god. Now is the time to experience the pleasantries of the athame. Prick your index finger and allow two drops of blood to hit the ground. No more, or else you can attract unwanted visitors. You should probably have a bandage handy as well so you can keep from getting blood everywhere. As you drop the blood on the ground, say this chant.

Mother Goddess, Father God

I ask you to bless this night

Fill this circle with your protection

Fill it full with your might

Grace me, please

as I bind my spells

in a book of shadows

help me do it well.

Keep it safe

from those who mean harm

make this book

a powerful charm.

Thank you for joining me

on this blessed night

give me strength to bless this book

give me strength to do it right.

After you call upon the deities, it is time to start the spell. First, you take the charged crystal and wave it over the book in three clockwise circles. As you wave the crystal chant.

Protect this vessel of my spells

keep it safe and keep it well

You should say the chant one time each time you make a circle, so three times total. Saying this will begin the portal of protection, and makes a gateway between the magic and your book to begin the protection spell.

Light your smudge stick, and after it is fully ignited, blow the flame out and leave it smoldering. Place the stick in the fireproof bowl and step away towards the altar towards the element air's candle. As you step towards air, chant this phrase:

Mighty power I ask you, please

open this spell and assist me

in protecting my secrets

and guarding my thoughts.

Repeat this chant as you move around the circle to each element. After you finish with spirit, waft the smoke over your spell book, and the pentacle at the same time. Waft it three times, and then pick up the pentacle, and press it on the cover of the book and say this phrase:

Protect this, oh Father and Mother

Protect this sacred book

So I ask may it be done.

57

After you have done that, you may thank the deities for joining you. After you part with the deities, you can close your circle, thanking each element as you dismiss it. Make sure that you put out your smudge stick and dispose of it in an environmentally friendly way. Now that your book of shadows has been blessed, you can use it to put your spells in.

Common Misconceptions about the Book of Shadows.

There are many different misconceptions about a Wiccan's book of shadows. Many people believe that there is one magical book of shadows that is constantly changing and holds all of the spell and answers of the universe. However, this is highly unlikely, because that much power would be easy to spot, and that much power is enough to turn even the purest Wiccan—evil. Power does not become a love until you experience it. More than likely, someone stumbled upon a powerful witch's book and felt that it was the all-powerful book.

Another misconception is that when you have a book of shadows, you have to have the same journal all of your life. Most witches book of shadows is actually a collection of journals that they have filled up throughout the year.

Unless you can find a giant book to keep, you are going to have to use more journals than you ever thought possible. This means that you are going to have to bless your new one every time, but don't worry, this does not take the blessings off your other books. Many witches use more than ten books in their lifetimes. Be careful not to have any loose papers in them; they will not be protected if they ever fall out of the book.

If you think of the spell and you are not around your book of shadows, you can write it down on loose paper, but be sure to transfer it to your book of shadows, don't just stuff sheets of paper in it.

Also, try to keep your spells organized. This can span from just organizing each book with different types of spells, to keeping separate books for different types of spells. Make sure to write the dates that you recorded the spells so you can see your progress over time as well. You want to have a well organized book so that when you need a spell, you can find it easily.

Many people think that books of shadows are super neat and only filled with completed spells. This is not true. Many of them have half finished spells, spells where things are crossed out and rewritten, spells that make no sense. In all honesty, a lot of witches even put their speculations and reactions from the spells in their books. These are essentially books to record your adventure through this life. If you see a witch with a perfect and pristine book of shadows, then they have probably transferred all of their old books into a new book to keep the appearance of knowing what they are doing. These people are often not witches, and at times, frauds. In some occasions, some witches do have OCD, and that explains their nearly perfect book of shadows. Like it is said, "don't trust a skinny cook," well, you shouldn't trust a pristine book of shadows either.

There is this hidden stigma that you should never let anyone see your book of shadows, and that is partially right, however, if you are in a coven or circle, chances are you are going to need to use it at some point. The actual danger is if another witch gets a hold of your book of shadows. That is why most witches try to hide theirs—to keep others from wanting to use it. However, if you just take care of it, and make sure that you know where it is at all times, you can show your friends in the Wiccan community.

Section One

Love and Relationship Spells

Introduction to Relationship Spells

There are many spells out there that you can use to help you find love and make strong bonds. These spells are great to have in your life, as they can do anything from giving you the confidence to approach someone, to attracting the right people into your life. There are spells for friendships as well, and you can make people drawn to you.

This magic comes at a price. You cannot force someone to fall in love with you; you can only influence them to do so by causing infatuation. You may find that once the spell wears off, so do their feelings for you. However, if you are not careful, you can cause them to have a powerful, and even dangerous obsession for you. Ask yourself, is it worth the possible side effects? Also, if you try to force someone to fall in love with you, you are making a moral mistake. This can cause some serious issues in some Wiccan communities. Love spells should only be used to attract the right people to you and to strengthen your bond with someone you already love.

If you are already in a committed relationship with someone, and you are both Wiccan, try casting a love spell together. This is a great way to bond well with your partner and keep the love alive. You are not doing anything wrong either because a love spell with someone you are already with is not forcing them to fall in love with you. It is inviting them to fall even more in love with you than they already are.

Love spells boost your confidence and can have you positively love yourself. Most Wiccans are so beaten down by the world because they see more than others do. They give more of themselves than the world deserves. And eventually, run out of love for themselves. This means that they may have problems in future relationships. A love yourself spell will bring that self-love back into your life. Once you love yourself again, it will be easier to love others who are around you, and give them the encouragement that they need, because you will feel that those words you are speaking are true. You must love yourself to love others.

You also can't force someone to be your friend. However, it is entirely possible to use a spell that will attract the right people in your life. The people that will lift you up whether they are under a spell or not. These are the people who you will want to be friends with your entire life. Friendship spells are great because then you can be sure that you are befriending the right people. If you do not target someone that you think would be a good friend, and instead let the great deities choose like it is meant to be. You want to find the right friends, not ones who are going to do you harm.

There are many love spells out there, and I am putting several different types in this section, to help you build your book of shadows in the love section. You can choose as many or as few as you would like to put in your book of shadows, or you can use these to try to create your own spells.

Love Spells

Many spells can help you find confidence in yourself. Confidence is an important part of love spells. If you have no confidence in yourself, then you can have some serious trouble with being able to help others, and as a Wiccan, part of your moral duty is to help others when they are having trouble. And, to find your true love, you must have confidence in yourself. This way you can show your true self and not miss an opportunity.

These spells can also help you find clarity and peace of mind. Some of them are herb spells, and some of them are just spells. Some of them you can do at any time of the day or night or year, but some are more specific. Some you don't even need a circle for. You can choose any of these spells that are in this book, or you can try to use your own. Don't underestimate your power just because you are beginning. If you want to try a few of these first, go ahead.

It is your book; it is your religion, it is you. You are in control. Now with that boost of confidence, let us move onto the actual spells, shall we?

First Date Confidence Charm

How many times have you been asked out on a date? If the answer is not very many, which is may be the case as Wiccans are known to be solitary people, then you probably get nervous during those first dates that you go on, which can hurt your chances of getting a second date.

First date jitters can cause you to stutter over the simplest words, or be unable to perform simple tasks properly. Ever knock something over, by accident, because you were nervous? If you freeze up in a nerve-wracking situation, the awkward silences can be what get you.

That is where a confidence charm comes into play. Note that some confidence charm spells could cause issues, as some may cause you to talk too much, to boast a lot, or to become obnoxious almost. You need one that is geared towards a first date. That is where this charm comes into play.

You don't need anything special, as this is just a simple charm. However, if you feel you need a little boost, you can smell some crushed borage to give you a confidence boost on top of the charm. Keep the smelling short as too much will be overbearing.

This charm is not permanent, so you want to use it, before your date, and if the date goes on for more than an hour, then you may want to "reapply" so to speak. If you are not ready to let your date in on your Wiccan ways excuse yourself to the restroom, and you can do it in the mirror there.

What you need

yourself

- ⚚ a mirror
- ⚚ a pinch of crushed borage (optional)

Just before your date, go to your bathroom, or any room with a mirror. If you have your borage, take three good whiffs of it now. Then look yourself in the eye in the mirror and say

I call upon your forces three

Let me see the worth of me

Confidence is what I seek

I am strong; I am not meek.

Say this three times in the mirror, and then enjoy your date. If you feel you're starting to lose confidence, say the charm again in a mirror. It doesn't matter if it is a big mirror or a pocket-sized mirror. You may want to practice this a few times before your date as well, this way the charm will be effective.

Love Yourself Spell

It is important to love yourself so that you can choose the love you truly deserve. Too often, we choose the love that we think we deserve, which is way under the love we actually deserve. This love that we choose is often way beneath what we deserve. You must love yourself enough to tell yourself that you deserve better than what is available at that second. That is what this spell is for. It will help you love yourself so that you can truly find the love you deserve.

What you need

- pink candle
- charged crystal pendant
- athame

This spell is a little weird, but it is one that I have found very effective. You are going to have to prick your finger, so bring a bandage along as well, so that you do not end up bleeding much and ruining the spell.

As this is an actual spell, you are going to have to do it during a moon phase. That is the new moon phase. This is the time of refreshing and changing some things in your life. You want to be fresh and new when you start to love yourself.

You are also going to have to cast a circle around your altar. This will be how you begin your spell. After you have finished opening your circle, step up to the altar. You need not invoke the Horned God, or Mother Goddess for this spell, just the elements. However, you still need to prick your finger. Drop a drop of blood on the pink candle, as close to the wick as you can get. Let the blood soak into the wick before you light the candle. Once most of the blood is soaked up, light the candle. Let it burn for ten minutes, while you think good thoughts about yourself while staring into the flames, blinking as little as you possibly can. You should feel yourself go into a trance like state. This is what you want.

DO NOT LET ANY BAD THOUGHTS IN.

It is imperative that you keep your thoughts good and pure to let the magic do its job successfully. If you have any bad thoughts about yourself seep in, then you will have to start the ten minutes over again. Once you have successfully gone three minutes with good thoughts, blow the candle out so that it is smoking. Take your crystal pendant and wave in three circles as you say this chant.

I am powerful, I am Pure, and I am bright

I ask the elements to show me so

I deserve to love myself

with a love greater than I have ever known.

Say this chant with every circle. Then after you finish that, put the pendant on, necklace style, and close your eyes. Place your dominant hand over your pendant, and recite this spell.

Love is power and might

I wish to have this power

Not only for others,

but for myself.

I deserve to be loved

not only by others

but by myself.

I want to love hard

not only others

but also myself

After you do this, you can close your circle. Make sure to thank the elements.

It sounds like a self motivation mantra, but this spell works wonders. It takes about two days for the full effect of the spell to take hold, but then you will begin noticing that you look in the mirror with a smile more often. Once the effects take place, you will find yourself saying no to people who are not willing to love you as much as you deserve. Learn that you have to take care of you before you can take care of anyone else. And you won't feel guilty about taking some time for yourself.

Removing Negative Attachments

Chances are, you probably have people in your life that you shouldn't be there and that makes it hard for the love yourself spell to take effect. So, you have to get rid of those people in your life. Easier said than done, right? This can be extremely hard if they have been around for a long time. Don't quit on them cold turkey, but if they're truly negative people or influences, then you can slowly remove them from your life.

Get rid of any bad habits that you have that could hold you back by making you feel bad about yourself. The only problem is that if you develop them over the course of several years, it is not that easy to drop them overnight.

This spell will help you remove all the things that are toxic in your life. Use it when you have to let go of your negative attachments. It is not a full out spell. You need to smudge yourself with a few things and say a few lines. No circle needed.

What you need

- black cohosh
- basil
- aloe
- fireproof bowl

Once you have a smudge stick made from the ingredients above, find a calming place for yourself and sit in a meditation pose. Before you smudge yourself, you should meditate and think of all the unhealthy things that you need to let go. Gather them all up in one "room" in your mind. Once you've done so, have everything together and light the smudge stick. Blow it out till it is smoldering and waft the smoke around you. With every wave of the smoke imagine more and more or your negativity and bad habits leaving.

As you imagine all the toxicity leaving your body, chant this phrase over and over until you feel refreshed.

Mind and body

heart and soul

they are not worth it

let it all go

Once you have finished doing this, you can open your eyes, and return to your normal activities. This serves you best during a new moon, but it can be performed at any time in the moon phases and still work.

Choose Peace Spell

Peace is something that we all need in our everyday life. We need to learn to choose peace to become non-confrontational. If you are less likely to start a confrontation, you will lead a happier life, and make stronger bonds with people, as you will be able to talk things out, rather than scream or be irrational.

If you are peaceful, you will be able to think a lot more clearly. Especially in troublesome situations. As a witch, it is important that you can assess a situation and find the proper spell with ease, so be peaceful.

This is a spell, so you will need a circle. However, it is not an intense one that requires any bloodletting. You also do not need any herbs for this. Know how to recite a spell easily and know how to make a circle.

Since you don't need anything other than what you use to cast a circle, let's just jump straight to the spell. You already know how to call the elements to cast a circle. After it is cast stand in the middle and say this spell.

I am not what hurt me

I am not the anger that surrounds me

I choose peace in all situations.

Elements surround me

protect my mind

help me choose peace every time.

After you have said this spell, you can close your circle. Say the spell as many times as you feel you need to before you close your circle.

Friendship is Important Too

A lot of people do not equate friendship with love. These people do not understand that no one can have the same type of love for you as your best friend does. Not even a significant other. It is important to have friends who care about you, and who love you, just as it is important for you to love yourself. You want friends who have your best interest at heart. These friends will usually tell you what you need to hear and not what you want to hear. For example, when they tell you, that person is no good for you, proceed with caution. These types of people are hard to come by.

You must have friendship in your life to truly complete yourself. While you do not need a lot of friends, you do need one or two good ones. People who will inspire you to be you, and not someone else. You should find friends that you want to be with you through your experience here on earth. From meeting the person of your dreams to walking down the aisle, these friends will be there for you through your journey here. And twenty years down the road, you will look back at all the fun times you had, and how close you still are and smile.

There are lots of friendship spells; I'm going to address the most common and popular spells.

Spell for New Friendships

Sometimes, we look around us and realize that people we thought were friends, were not truly friends, or that we have drifted apart from friends, and realize we need new connections—ones that will last. Wiccans tend to be introverted and sometimes have a harder time connecting with people. This spell is a little different than the spells we have covered, but it is not drastically different.

What you need

- ribbon or yarn (enough to make a bracelet)
- yellow candle
- good luck oil

To begin, gather your supplies, and cast your circle. You will want to put a drop of the oil on the candle to anoint it before you light it. Start to braid the yarn into a friendship bracelet. As you are braiding say this spell.

Intertwine and interwoven

May our friendship not be broken

truest friends, attract to me

so I will, so it must be

Repeat this spell until you have finished your bracelet. Then you should add three drops of the oil to the bracelet, then wrap the bracelet around the candle until it burns out. Once the candle burns out, take the bracelet and put it on. Finally, close your circle, and thank each element as it departs.

Charm for Spiritual Connections

This is more of a chant than a spell, so you do not have to cast a circle. You are merely putting out good thoughts in the atmosphere to find a deep spiritual connection with someone. These people can be friends or other loved ones. Spiritual connections are important because you need someone who sparks your soul.

When you have the time, go into a solitary room, and shut yourself away. Think about the type of connection you want, and close your eyes. You want to find something deep within your interests, so keep that in mind. While you are imagining, the connection say this chant.

My heart my soul my spiritual friend

come to me I welcome you in.

Say the chant three times and then open your eyes. You have completed the chant. Now go out there and talk to people. Soon you will find someone who sparks your very spirit. Be willing to get out there and find the person. This spell will also do its part and will draw you to the right people.

Apple Divination Spell

Divination is a great way to tell the true intentions of those around you. You can also use it to find love. Whether it be true love or friendship, divination can help you find it all. I know the Harry Potter realm kind of laughed at the topic of divination, by casting a crazy lady as the professor who taught it. However, it is a real spell and should be taken seriously.

What you need

- ⚔ an apple
- ⚔ an apple peel
- ⚔ a boiling pot of hot water

To begin, peel an apple in a circular motion, making an unbroken spiral. As you peel, say this chant.

Apple peel, please let us play a game,

take the form of the first initial of my true friend's first name

75

The mysteries of love, and the joy of Halloween

Using the help of Pomona

make your symbol clear to me

After you have said the chant, toss the peel over your shoulder into the water (this may take some practice). Then, as it heats up, the peel will unfurl, taking the shape of the first letter of the first name of the person you are searching for.

Love and Romance

Finally, the section you may have been waiting for. True love magic. Everyone wants, and deserves, to find their true love. These spells will help you find the love you deserve. Using these spells, however, may not always have the best effects if you use them with the wrong intentions.

Have good intentions if you want to attract true love, not the love you think you want. As was stated in the beginning, you cannot force someone to fall in love with you, and trying to do so can be disastrous. Let the right person fall in love with you. Doing otherwise will have you chasing someone for years and missing out on the right person— talk about wasting time.

Quality Attraction Charm

You want to attract a quality relationship. The higher quality the relationship, the better you will connect, and the closer you will be to true love.

This charm involves a talisman of sorts in the form of perfume or cologne.

What you need

- ⚔ your favorite perfume or cologne
- ⚔ carnation oil

To use this charm, take a bottle of your favorite eau de toilette and add a few drops of carnation oil. This will cause it to attract pure love to you. After you add the oil, say this chant.

As I will so mote it be

bring me, love of quality

That is all you have to do for this one. Whenever you go out, spritz the charmed spray on yourself, and watch it work its magic. You will soon find someone who is worth being in a relationship with.

Romance Attraction Smudge

Everyone wants romance in their life. Romance is what keeps love alive. If you want romance in your life, this smudge will help you do attract it.

What you need

- apple
- carnation
- chickweed
- chili
- cinnamon
- violet
- wallflower
- hyacinth
- white candle
- fireproof bow

Create, or buy, a smudge stick with these ingredients (minus the white candle) Once you have a properly dried the smudge stick, it is time to start the ceremony.

Take the smudge stick, and light it with the white candle. Blow out the fire on the stick, and lay it in a fireproof bowl. Waft the smoke over you, and say this chant

Light of passion

build my fire

fill my relationship with desire

After you have said the chant four or five times and smudged yourself fully, you can put out and dispose of the smudge stick. Happy romancing!

Ritual Bath for a Blind Date

This magic is a bit different. This involves taking a bath. However, you have to cast a circle. Do not worry about being naked in the presence of the goddess, for in the Wiccan culture, it is natural not to be covered. You are free to be as you please. During this bath, you need to focus on relaxing and letting all the stress melt from your body. You want to be fresh and renewed to allow the positivity to flow through you.

Because this is a blind date, you also want to be extra alert to your inner feelings. That is imperative because you do not know the person at all. If there is something off about them, then you want to be able to get out before you are in danger. Next, you want to be protected. Be careful, but don't be worried. You want to be confident and strong. That is what this bath is for. It will give you the protection, clarity, and confidence you need to make this date a success or to get out before things go bad.

What you need

- a bathtub
- water to temp
- rose petals
- chamomile
- blue flag iris
- cinnamon oil

- ⚜ centaury
- ⚜ basil
- ⚜ blue candle
- ⚜ red candle
- ⚜ yellow candle
- ⚜ green candle
- ⚜ purple candle

In this ritual, you do not have to light the candles around yourself in a circle, as being in a tub makes it hard. Make a circle beside the tub with candles. Fill your bath with water at the temperature of your choice until it is at a suitable height for you. Add the rose petals, chamomile, blue flag iris, and basil in your water. Anoint the candles with the cinnamon oil before you light them and open your circle (do not put cinnamon in your bath as it is an irritant).

Climb into your bath and relax. Feel the effects of all the herbs in the bath take place. This is the time when you purify yourself and ready yourself for the upcoming date. It is best to do this as close to your date as possible, so the effects don't wear off. It lasts for around twenty-four hours. If you do so the morning of your date, you should be perfectly fine.

Once you have finished your bath (take the time to let the water get cold), you can close your circle, and get on with your day.

Section 2

Wealth and Prosperity Spells

Introduction to Wealth and Prosperity Spells

We all need some wealth and prosperity in our lives, and that's okay. Sometimes we are a little short on cash, and there is nothing wrong with wanting a little help. This is totally normal, and there are even spells to help you become successful in your business, and money making endeavors. With these spells, you may find yourself with a little more abundance of wealth than you thought possible.

I must warn you, though, that you should not be greedy. While prosperity is one thing, you should not try to use spells to make money if you do not want to put in the effort. These spells should be used entirely to supplement the income you already make. You also should not hoard the money that you make. Prosperity is only truly noticed when you spread it around. Help the little old lady down the street have a more successful garden, give the next door neighbor little financial surprise to help with Christmas. It doesn't have to be a lot, just spread the love around.

That being said there are a few spells that are good to use without causing you to be greedy. They fill your crops, and your piggy bank to help you become more successful.

These spells will help you find coins and other loose inconsequential money just laying around. If you do happen to find bigger bills, then your belief and power are stronger than most beginners. However, if you know whose money it is, then you should absolutely give it back. If there is no one around, then that money was meant for you.

Success and Prosperity Spells

These spells relate to your success and giving you prosperity in your endeavors. These do not always bring you access to random bouts of money, but open the gates to making the money that you need, and making sure that you prosper in your garden and businesses.

Everyone wants to succeed at what they do, and if you use these spells, they will help you gain success. However, they will not keep you on the success ladder forever; you have to buck up and put in the effort to remain successful. You cannot rely on magic to do all your work for you.

Garden Planting Spell

If you are a gardener, chances are you want your crops to succeed and be bountiful. This spell helps for that. This spell is to be done while you are planting your garden, to give it a successful chance from the time the seeds hit the ground. This spell is a little different than the ones that we have listed so far, but it is a good one, and it has been shared by many witches.

What you need

- ⚶ 2 wooden stakes for each row of your garden

- ⚶ 1 piece of pastel ribbon for each stake

- ⚶ small tree or bush branch with new leaves

- ⚶ 2 qt. container

- ⚶ seeds or plants

- ⚶ 1 qt. milk

- ⚶ ½ cup of honey

Mix the milk and honey, and pour it into the container. Stick the branch in the container, leaves down.

Take all of the materials outside. As you start a row of seeds or plants, stick a stake in the ground at the head of that row and tie a piece of ribbon on it. As you tie the ribbon on, say this phrase

Sprout and thrive with life anew

with this perfect love, I give to you

When you finish a row, repeat the stake/ribbon/chant step, and continue with every row. You should say the chant two times with every row you do one for each stake with ribbon you put in the ground.

After you have planted your garden, grab the milk mixture and go back to the beginning row. Take the branch and use it to sprinkle the mixture across each row while saying this spell

Milk and honey flow throughout

Fertilize each seed and sprout

Sprites of the garden, dance, and play

Twirl and laugh in my garden each day

Bring large growth and abundance to this spot

Everywhere you dance, play and walk

After you do this, water your garden, and tend to it daily.

Honey Abundance Jar

This is a ritual that is kind of strange if you think about it, but it really works. It started as a hoodoo ritual, and spread to the Wiccan culture, as it has shown to be very successful.

The honey abundance jar is a way for you to welcome prosperity into your life. If you do so, you will find things get better with time.

What you need

- Honey
- a pinch of chamomile
- a pinch of Irish moss
- a hinge lidded jar
- a pinch of cinnamon
- money drawing oil
- a small piece of paper
- a pen
- a small green candle
- matches

To begin, write out what you are looking for. Is it a new job, a second income? Make sure when you are writing, your pen never leaves the paper. Even if you are starting a new word, just drag the pen over. Continuity is key here.

After you do that, you put the paper in the jar. Cover the paper with leaves, and pour the honey over it. Close and secure the lid of the jar.

Now you rub the money oil into your candle and then light it. Let a few drops of the wax drip onto the lid of the jar, and use that wax to secure the candle to the lid. Then, let the candle burn out completely in one shot. Repeat this process once a month, and you will be surprised at the difference it makes.

Moonlight Prosperity Spell

This money spell is to be done by the full moon, to give you the fullest amount of power to the spell. You want to do so when the moon is at its peak, which means staying up a little late. Most Wiccans find that they are night owls, so it shouldn't be a problem for you.

What you need

- cauldron

- water

- silver coin

- full moon

Once you have everything ready, cast a circle around your cauldron. After your circle is cast, take the water and pour it into your cauldron till the cauldron is half full. Once that is done, slip the silver coin into the water.

Waving your hands over the water as if you are trying to scoop up the silver of the moon's reflections, say this chant three times.

Moon Goddess hear my cry

Bring me prosperity on this night

Let me use it well and wise

to keep that prosperity my whole life

After you have finished this, you can close your circle, and pack up your things.

Interview Success Charm

This is extremely simple and doesn't require a chant.

- physical photo of yourself

- green candle

- dollar bill

- paperclip

Light the candle, and take the dollar bill and wave both sides of it to the flame. Once you do this, blow out the candle, and paperclip the money to the photo of yourself. Carry this in your purse or wallet to your interview.

Business Success Charm

This is also a very easy charm to do, though it does take some talking.

What you need

- a strand of silver jingle bells

Hold the bells and say this chant

Bells song bring me luck

and great prosperity all year long

Hang the bells on the door of your business, and every time it rings it shall bring success.

Money Attractants

Cinnamon Money Charm

This spell is to attract just money to you. The money may not be substantial, but should definitely give you a boost.

What you need

- ⋏ ground cinnamon

- ⋏ dollar bill

- ⋏ belief

This spell must be done on a Thursday as this is the strongest time of the week for money spells.

Dampen the dollar bill on both sides with a little water. Then wet your finger, and dip it in the cinnamon. Make three lines with the cinnamon on the dollar bill, and then place it where you would normally keep your money. Be sure to believe that this works, and watch the money start rolling in.

Pyrite for Prosperity

This is a different type of magic. Crystal magic to be exact. Crystal magic is the art of pairing crystals together to get the effect you want. In this spell, we are using pyrite to attract wealth. There are other crystals that attract wealth, but Pyrite is the strongest.

Crystal magic is easy, but it does take some faith for it to be a success. You first charge your crystals with what you want from them. In above spells, you read that you need to charge a clear quartz crystal to do the spell. However, there was no instruction on how to charge a crystal. A guide is in order.

To charge a crystal, you first hold it tightly in your hand and "make a wish" your wish can be anything, though certain crystals work best with certain crystals. For wealth and prosperity, citrine, green aventurine, tiger's eye, moss agate, ruby, jade, and pyrite are the best. When you want to use a crystal, simply make your wish while holding it tight with your eyes closed, and leave it in the light of a full moon overnight.

Once charged they are ready. Keep in mind, even if unused, the charges do not last forever and should be renewed once a month at every full moon. It is always a good idea to charge a plethora of crystals. If you do not have a specific wish for your crystals, and just want to charge them to use for future spells, then simply leave them in the light of the full moon, and they will charge with a neutral power. Charge as many or as few crystals as you like, however, the more that you charge, the more prepared you will be in the future. I often have ten to twelve crystals charging every full moon.

What you need

- ⅄ one pyrite crystal

- ⅄ eight other wealth crystals of your choice

- ⅄ belief

To begin, charge your crystals during a full moon. Once they are charged, arrange them in a circle with pyrite in the middle. Place these crystals in a safe but well-trafficked area in your home. Such as a high shelf in your living room or bedroom. The crystals will work their magic on your home, and you will soon be blessed with prosperity. Make the crystals remain standing daily. You want to get the most out of your crystals as possible, and if any of them have broken formation, they will cause issues in the magic stream.

These are some money spells and charms to welcome money and prosperity in your life. Remember not to be greedy, and to spread the wealth around.

Section 3

Health and Well Being Spells

Introduction to Health and Well Being Spells

Everyone wants to be healthy, and have a good, healthy life. Unfortunately, life has other plans. With flu, injuries, and death all trying to sneak up on you, these spells are evergreen. Health and wellbeing spells keep you in general good health. You can't repair a broken bone or an injured spleen, but you can ward off the flu, and relieve minor injuries.

I must warn you, that you cannot bring someone back from the dead. Cannot. Cannot. Cannot. Some of the greatest witches of all time have lost their minds trying. Nicholas Flamel, the world's most famed alchemist, went crazy because he created a stone to resurrect the dead, and the results drove him insane. You probably heard that name before, if nowhere else, but the Harry Potter world in the first book, *Harry Potter and the Sorcerer's Stone.* The Philosopher's Stone was said to keep the person in possession alive for as long as they were in possession of the stone. What the book didn't mention was that the stone could also bring back the dead. However, that was mentioned in the *Deathly Hallows*, and Ian Peverell, the receiver of the resurrection stone, went crazy.

Keep that in mind—just a fair warning. Moving on, only use healing spells for what they are meant to do. Heal minor injuries. There is no magical potion to regrow or heal broken bones in a night, and there is no way to repair an organ, either. Trying to do so could have devastating results.

Because healing spells are at a higher than beginner level, there are no actual injury healing spells in this section. They take a lot of energy, and if not done right, they can be disastrous, so it is best that you save those until you have had more practice with higher level spells. In this section, there are spells to do with personal health and your well being. Such as protection and mental health.

Health

Speedy Recovery Bath

If you are injured, or not feeling well, chances are you want to recover fairly quickly. This spell will speed up the recovery period and get you back on your feet sooner. It is not an immediate healing spell, but it will speed up the process.

What you need

- ⚕ angelica

- ⚕ arnica

- ⚕ castor oil

- ⚕ chamomile

- ⚕ yellow candle

- ⚕ purple candle

- ⚕ bathtub

- ⚕ water to temperature liking

To begin, fill the tub with water to the temperature of your liking, to a water-level suitable for you. Dump in angelica, arnica, and chamomile (as much as you think you need). Let the herbs soak in the water. While they are doing that, anoint the candles with castor oil, and light them. Turn off the lights, and get in the bath, soaking until the water starts to get cold. While you are soaking, let your mind relax, and drift away to your happy place. Imagine your body being whole, and nothing ails you. Once you get out of the bath, blow out the candles, and continue with your day.

Anxiety Calming Spell

Anxiety is a common problem in Wiccans. This is due to their empathic sensitivities. If you find yourself having an anxiety attack, you can use this spell to help you. Anxiety can strike at any time; thus, this spell is created to have all of the effects of an anxiety spell, without a lot of ingredients. The only thing you need is a few minutes of peace.

To do this spell find a quiet place, if you are in public and can't wait—the restroom should suffice. Get as close to the floor as you can, and curl up into a meditation pose. Take three deep breaths and say this chant

Anxiety

leave me be

take your leave

and be gone from me

Say this chant ten times. Watch as your anxiety disappears and you can have fun even in the most crowded of situations.

Yellow Infusion Pick Me Up Spell

Everyone needs a pick me up spell, this one uses the color yellow, which is a known mood lifter to make you feel better.

What you need

- yellow candle

- yellow ribbon (enough for a bracelet)

- yellow paper (very small piece)

- yellow marker

- castor oil

To begin, anoint the candle with castor oil and let the oil seep into the candle. While the oil sets, take the yellow marker and write on the yellow paper how you wish to feel. Whether you want to feel happy, excited, or joyous use cursive, and don't lift the marker from the page until you are done. Once you have the word written down, make your bracelet by braiding the ribbons together. As you braid, say this spell.

Little bracelet

so intricately made

braided by hand

made by me

take my mood

lift me up

make me feel better soon

Say this as many times as it takes to get the bracelet braided. After you have braided the bracelet, set it to the side. Take the candle and light it. Stick the paper in the flame, and let it burn up. Once the paper burns entirely, grab the bracelet and blow out the candle. Then hold the bracelet in the smoke until the smoke dissipates. Put the bracelet on, and feel your mood start to brighten.

Red Jasper for Energy and Endurance

Energy and endurance are necessities of life. Especially if you are an active person. This spell will help you keep up your energy and help you do those tasks that you have been wanting to do but just never seem to have the time or the energy to do at the end of the day. Or it can help you run that marathon that you signed up for. Whatever you need that requires energy, this spell works.

This spell requires the use of the chakras. You must first locate your base (root) chakra which is located at the base of your spine—a quick search online will depict it clearer.

What you need

- ⚹ a tad of chakra knowledge

- ⚹ red jasper stone

To begin, locate your base chakra. You must be entirely relaxed for this to work. Take the red jasper stone, and place it on your base chakra, and imagine the energy flowing through you. Say this spell

Stone of energy

spare me some

fill me up

and make me run

Once you have done that, rest for fifteen minutes with the stone on your chakra. Repeat the process two more times. After the third time's rest period is over, you can then continue with your day.

Well Being Spells

Pet Protection Collar

If you have pets, then more than likely, you want to protect them. But what happens if you aren't around to protect them. We can't be home every minute of every day to watch them. That is what this spell is for. This spell will adhere to your dog's collar. It is actually a smudge of the collar with protective herbs.

What you need

- bay

- angelica

- blessed thistle

- basil

- pet collar

To begin, get a smudge stick created from the four herbs mentioned above. You know the drill by now. Find a quiet room, light the stick, blow it out to a smolder. However, you do not want to place it in a bowl. You want the ashes from the stick to fall on the collar. Wave the smudge stick over the collar several times while chanting

Mother Goddess protect my friend

from all harm until the end

Keep chanting this until the smudge stick has burned well over halfway down. Once you have done this, you can put out the stick, and rub the ashes into the collar. Clean up your mess, and let the collar sit overnight with the ashes rubbed into it. Wash and dry the collar, and then put it on your pet. The collar will now provide your pet with the protection he or she needs.

Witch Bottle for Home Protection

This bit of magic will provide a protective field around your home so that even when you are away your home is protected from bad happenings.

What you need

- an empty wine bottle

- small blue taper candle

- blessed thistle

- paper

- pen

- cats eye stone (small)

To begin, take the bottle, and wash it out. Make sure that it is clean. Once the bottle is clean, take the piece of paper and pen, and write what you want from the jar (protection of the household is a good place to start). Make sure once you start writing, the pen doesn't leave the paper until you are finished. Stick the paper in the bottle, and cover with blessed thistle and the cat's eye stone. Cork the bottle back up, and light the candle. Use a few drops of wax to secure the candle to the cork, and then let the candle burn out. Once it has burnt out, put the bottle in your living room to protect the whole house. Do this once a month.

Morning Motivation Potion

If you are anything like me, it is hard to get moving in the morning, and coffee itself doesn't always help. However, this potion can do the trick.

What you need

- coffee

- aloe (1 tsp per 12 cups)

- cayenne (just a pinch!)

- centaury (less than a tsp)

Make every morning like you would regular coffee, and watch the motivation kick in.

Section 4

Assorted Spells

Introduction to Assorted Spells

There are many other useful spells to help in everyday life that don't pertain to a specific category of spells. These spells range from basic to advanced. In this book, we are only going to focus on the basic ones. As you become more proficient, you can move on to more difficult spells. There will be more difficult spells in the next book *Wicca: Herbal Magic*.

Spells

Elemental Blessing for the New Year

This is a spell to bless your new year.

What you need

- athame

- cauldron

- water

Cast a circle, and once you have done that, stand at the altar with your cauldron. Pour the water into the cauldron.

Take your athame and prick your finger. Do not bandage your finger. Stick your pricked finger and dip it in the water swirling it around. Say this spell

Blessed One in the Sky

see my new year

Give me success

rid me of fear

make it great

oh, blessed God.

Close your circle and thank the elements.

Clarity Spell

This spell is to clear your mind and give you clarity.

Cast your circle, and say this chant

Brain on fire

with questions alight

clear yourself

get it right

Close your circle and thank the elements.

Avocado Beauty Spell

This is a spell to brighten your skin up and bring forth your inner beauty.

What you need

- avocado

- chamomile

Mix the two ingredients together, and apply to your face. Let sit for thirty minutes. Before you remove say this spell

Beauty within

Beauty without

clear my skin

don't make me shout

make me bright

shiny and new

as I say

I ask of you

Remove the mixture from your face, and wash your face thoroughly.

Wicca

Herbal Magic

A Beginner's Guide to Mastering Wiccan Herbal Magic with Herb Spells

Valerie W. Holt

Section 1

The Ancient Art of Herbalism

Introduction to Herbalism

Herbalism is a very common and core part of paganism. It was used way back before paganism was even thought of. Herbs are a part of our everyday lives, as we use them to season our food, and add color to our plates, but did you know that herbs used to be all that was available as medicine? It's true. Back before modern medicine came into play, herbs were used to cure ailments. Well, that and bloodletting. Which is another common practice in magic rituals. Which makes me wonder why on earth they burned witches in the 19th century when all they were doing was killing their doctors (hmm..).

Anyways, back on topic, herbalism was adapted by the Wiccan religion and is used in a lot of spells. These spells range from luck spells to health and well-being spells. There is an herb that can do pretty much anything you need it to in a spell.

Herbs are used in smudge sticks, ritual baths, spells, and witch jars. They are a very important part of the Wiccan rituals, and chances are, in most spells, you will need to use at least one type of herb, or herb oil. There are so many things that herbs can be used for it is mind boggling. Most people don't give a second thought to the basil they are putting in their stew. They never even wonder what protective magic it is bestowing on them.

There are many people who used herbs in a variety of ways. These people existed before Wiccans and still, exist today. There are so many religions out there, and a majority of them use herbs in some way.

History of Herbalism

There are many different accounts of not only humans but animals with cognitive functioning using herbs to cure ailments. The Tanzanian chimp cures worms with the pith of the Veronian plant. Humans of the area do so as well. So humans are not the only ones who are known to use herbalism. Cats eat grass to settle their stomachs if they have indigestion. The type of grass they eat depends on the area they live in, and what's available.

Now on to the human history of herbalism. Humans have used herbalism since there were humans on the planet. Back when the cavemen roamed the earth, herbs were all they had to cure the ailments that they had. If they chose the wrong one, that could be disastrous. Since the beginning of time, people have relied on herbs for cures for sicknesses. It wasn't until the last hundred years that we really got into modern medicine.

There are even documentations that go back over fifty thousand years that show that people back then used herbs to cure sicknesses that arose over time. A lot of the herbs that they used then, we use today, though most of them are called by a different name, as plant names have changed over the season. Herbs are documented to have eased the passing of some people who were too far gone to save. And have even been known to stop the spread of yellow fever, if caught soon enough. Herbs were there throughout bouts of epidemics, the bubonic plague, the red death, so many other diseases have been combated by herbs until modern medicine came along and completely knocked them out.

Magic and Medicine

There is a lot of magic in the world. A lot of it is found in older style medicine. In the olden days, medicine was based on a lot of pagan magic. Medicine and magic have known to go hand in hand so much so, that a lot of really religious Catholics refused to see a doctor when they were sick, and would rather die than be touched by "wicked magic." A lot of them did die due to the complications and issues from their ailments.

Medicine was very different than it is today, as there were no pills. Whiskey and rum were prescribed as cough syrup, and marijuana was prescribed for aches and pains regularly. Basic herbs today were mixed up for potions, tonics, and poultices. While there was not always a spell said over the herbs, a lot of the tonics and potions were a lot like magic rituals done by shamans.

Shamanism and the Early Herbal Pioneers

Back before you were even thought of. Before your mother was even thought of, well, even before your grandmother was even thought of there were shamans and herbal pioneers. These people were in charge of taking care of the sick in a village and blessing young mothers, and anything else that needed herbal magic. These people were often revered, but in some cultures they were outcast. It all depends on if Roman Catholicism had made it to the area then.

There are many shamans in the world, and contrary to popular beliefs, they don't all live in the mountains of Indonesia. There are many in the United States, even in New York. Shamans are everywhere in the world, and they still are in practice today. They use herbs to tell your future, to heal you spiritually, and physically. They use herbs for so many things, and it is astounding how many ways they can help with nothing but what they find in the earth.

Shamans are always depicted as an old man who lives at the top of a mountain, but the truth is there are more Native American shamans than there are Indonesian shamans. It is actually a common practice for the natives to call upon their shamans, known as medicine men, to heal them. Some tribes still do not go to hospitals unless absolutely necessary. They choose to trust their own people, with good reason, but we are not going to get into politics in this book.

Medicine men are often tribe elders or a member of the elder's family. Sometimes the medicine men are actually women, but they are generally men, as women are seen as needed to take care of the children and the dwelling, and to cook for the men when they bring home the meat.

In Egypt, they were known to use herbalism to cure people and poison them. Herbalism was rampant in ancient Egypt, even being used as the first embalming techniques. These techniques were used to help keep the bodies preserved as well as possible because they believed that a decaying body was an invitation for the devil to steal the soul. So they made an archaic version of formaldehyde with plants that they found available to them.

Herbalism was used heavily in Saudi Arabia and still is today. There are many people in ancient history and history today that use herbs for medicinal purposes, and not for just food.

Many Meanings of *Herb*

There are many different meanings of the word herb. With so many different cultures out there, it makes sense that the translation may be a little different from group to group. Some groups are more closed on the meaning, and some are more open, it all depends on what is available in their area.

Only Grass & Branch Like

Some people only count the leafy plants as herbs. These are what a lot of people consider herbs. Thyme, basil, beech, thistle, and other branch like, leafy, green plants are classified as herbs.

Including Flowers

Some groups include flowers as herbs. Apple blossoms, chamomile, and carnation flowers are often used. Rose petals are used in a lot of Wiccan spells. Flowers can be just as useful as the green leafy plants that most people associate herbs with. You can use almost every type of flower out there for some part of a ritual.

Including Oils

This is something that very few groups do. Wiccans are a part of the select few. Oils can help in many different spells and healing balms. These groups find things such as castor oil and coconut oil useful. There are many other oils that are an essential part of the Wiccan culture as well.

Herbs in Practice

Herbs are an essential part of the Wiccan culture, as a lot of spells depend on a variety of herbs to be successful. Smudges are another thing that relies on herbs. In fact, smudge sticks are made up entirely of herbs. You take the herbs, roll them into a bundle, and then you light them and use the smoke to cleanse the area.

You can use oils on the object you wish to bless, or you can use it to anoint the candle you are using to do the ritual.

Flowers are very common as well. A Wiccan may use a combination of all three (herb, oils, flowers) in a spell as well. There is no limit to what you can do when you combine herbs.

You can use herbs in your everyday life as well, in common foods, and choose the herbs that you need for your day.

Herbs are very helpful in your food, and in your drinks to go on with your day. They mesh well with the human body and lifestyle.

Magical Power of Plants

The Power of Correspondence

This is not the type of correspondence you would see between friends. You don't write letters to your herbs. Herbal correspondence is literally how the herb talks to the world. Herbal correspondences refer to the workings of the herb, and how it reacts to the world around it (and other herbs).

Herbal correspondence is a very powerful thing, as it can literally change your entire day, and can make or break a spell. Knowing the correspondences will help you figure out if a spell is for protection, or if it is for wealth. It will also keep you from turning a spell about power into a humbling spell.

You want to know the correspondences of each herb that you work with, and some essential herbs will be listed in a later section for you to learn a little more about.

Intelligent Life on Earth

Humans are not the only form of intelligent life on earth. In fact, every species is intelligent in their own way. Just because they do not have the same reasoning skills as us, doesn't mean that they are not intelligent, and do not have their own hierarchy of cognitive skills. If they didn't, all dogs would have the same learning abilities, but as you will find, some dogs are smarter than others.

Herbs help the intelligent life on earth. Herbs help even the least responsive of intelligent creatures. They often use them for indigestion or other problems that bother them. Chimpanzees seem the most knowledgeable about herbs, using herbs for everything from worm reduction and cures to spreading banana on injuries to help speed up the healing process.

Plants themselves are considered intelligent life by some, as they feel what goes on around them. A tree actually feels pain, and a polygraph test can register the pain. That is how herbs work. They send their energy out into the atmosphere around you, and you use their energy to send a message out into the world to do what you need them to.

Section 2

Getting Acquainted with Herbs

Where to Start

We all have to start somewhere, so if you know nothing or very little about herbs, then you're at the right place. This section is going to cover the basics t about the main herbs that are used in Wiccan traditions. You will learn what they do and how to use them.

Before we begin, you have to find out where you are going to get your herbs. Is there a herb store near you that sells strange herbs that you can use in your spells? Do you have to order them online? Are you going to grow them yourself? These questions must be answered so that you can figure out the best option for you. For now, you might want to stick with buying the herbs at a store or online, unless you are experienced in gardening, and experienced with growing exotic herbs. Some herbs are hardier than others, but some are very delicate, and if not grown correctly, will not succeed in your spells.

Also, you must have a place to store your herbs. This could be a dark cabinet or a dresser. They should have a cool, dark place to be stored so that they do not get damp and moldy, and do not dry out too much. Dried is good, dry rot is not.

Find some information online about taking care of your herbs so that they will last you a long time, so you are not constantly having to buy new ones. You should also learn about how to crush leaves with a mortar and pestle properly.

Another thing that you should learn is how to make a smudge stick. I will put basic instruction here, but you can find more information online about how to make them.

Choose the herbs for the smudging that you need to do. Pick some that are roughly the same length, and lay them all out in a bundle. Get some natural twine or natural cotton (so that there are no harmful fumes when burned) and bind the smudge stick starting at the bottom and working your way up. If you can get away with only using three bindings, that is your best bet, because it exposes the most herbs while still being held well.

After you bind up the smudge stick, you have to dry it if the herbs are not already dry. To dry it, wrap it in paper, and change the paper every day for ten days. In ten days' time, you will have a dry smudge stick.

Thirteen Magical Herbs

While there are many herbs out there, and each of them have magical properties, there are some that are more pertinent than others, and these are the ones that we are going to discuss in this section. These herbs are part of a shaman's everyday work bag, and that every witch should keep a stock of in their store room. These herbs are an important part of your spells and just your everyday well-being. You should always have a stock of them on hand.

Basil

Basil is a herb that you often find in your local supermarket. It is a very strong, natural tasting herb that almost has a little bit of spice to it. It is green and leafy like. This herb gives you protection of the spirit. It is also used in a lot of home protection spells as well. It brings wealth while repelling negativity, and it is a sacred plant.

You want this plant in your home. It will bring you peace of mind knowing that its mystical powers are watching over you. Try making a smudge stick combined with some other herbs such as sage, and smudging your house with it to ward off any evil that may be lurking, and creating a protective shield over your household.

Basil is one of the most used herbs in spells due to its versatility. It is essential that you have a stock of it both crushed and full in your store room, and maybe keep a little around for quick access.

Bay Laurel

This is another green leafy herb like basil, but it has a bit of a sweeter taste. This herb is also really important and should be kept on hand. All of the herbs in this section should be kept on hand, but some more so than others. Basil and Bay Laurel are the important ones, along with Sage which is further down the line.

This little herb acts as the guardian of the household. It protects your family and wards of evildoers. It also protects you against illness and other ailments. No one wants to get sick, and the more you use this herb, the better health you will be in. Try putting it in a witch jar with a few other herbs that are listed in here and see how much better your life becomes.

When you burn these leaves, you'll find that it may produce visions. You have to be open to the visions, or else you will not get clear ones if any at all. However, if you relax your mind, you may get visions quite easily. They will come to you, so don't try to force them. Pay attention to the minute details of your vision, like a clock on the wall, what time it says. The calendar in the corner, and the date that is circled. These minute details are almost more important than the main scene in the vision because if you are meant to prevent, or cause something, you need to know when it should happen.

Chamomile

Chamomile is a herb that is very easily found. It is often used as a tea leaf and makes a very delicious cup of hot tea. It is very sweet, with just an air of bitterness on the back of the tongue. This combination of such starkly contrasting flavors is what makes it so desirable for people to drink. But this herb is more than just good for the popular beverage; it has other purposes as well.

It is great for meditation. It soothes the inner soul and keeps you grounded to the earth while you meditate. It pushes all of your inner troubling's away and calms you mentally and spiritually. This allows you to balance out your mind before you meditate. Try drinking a cup of chamomile tea with Valerian root sweetened with a little honey before your next meditation session.

This herb also attracts money and is often used in prosperity charms. When used in the right spells, it can attract a small amount of wealth to you, and when coupled with other wealth attractants, can attract even more wealth to you.

Chamomile is a great herb and is an easy one to use if you do not want to cast a circle and make a smudge stick. Just make a cup of tea, say your piece over it, and drink it.

Cinnamon

I am pretty sure everyone in the universe knows this beautiful and flavorful spicy stick. It is a holiday season must have for people of the Christian religion, but for Wiccans, it is so much more. This little doodad is a triple threat in the pantry if you know what I'm saying.

That's right. It is an aphrodisiac. It can draw someone close to you and is charged with romantic energy. And not just the hold your hand on a Saturday night type of romance. The whole nine yards romance. The type that people will be begging for more of.

But not only is it an aphrodisiac, it is also used to draw power and success to you. Use this in a spell about domination in the work place, and you might just achieve it if you have enough.

This small brown roll of energy is just what you need in your pantry to get life going the way you want it to be.

Dandelion

Dandelion, the tiny yellow plant that as it develops turns into nothing but fluffy white seeds. These little plants are mysterious in how they work. They start out beautiful, and then they turn into these cute white little puff balls that remind you of a bunny's tail, and if you blow on that puffball it spreads hundreds of seeds everywhere, and you make a wish for those seeds to carry away. At least that is what we are taught as children anyway.

In reality, dandelions don't grant wishes. They do, however, bring inner peace. You may find that your spirit calms when you blow on a dandelion, and you may even feel energized. That's because those are two of the main properties of this herb. As you blow on the dandelion, you are releasing its correspondences into the air.

Dandelions also enhance your prophetic powers. They do this through your dreams. Try putting a vase of them beside your bed (preferably while they are in the flowering phase, otherwise, you may have a mess.) When you go to bed, stare at the dandelions until you fall asleep. In the morning write down your dreams, and look for a pattern. You may have been blessed with a prophecy.

Elecampane

This herb is known for its healing properties. It is a root herb that is often used to clear up bronchial infections, but it has a lot of other wonderful well-being aspects to it as well.

It is great for protecting you from getting pneumonia, and it is used to strengthen the immune system. While it is not used for much outside the realm of protection, it is very important to have if you want to do a healing spell.

Hibiscus

Hibiscus is the beautiful flower that is commonly found in Hawaii. It is the cousin of the Lotus flower and is quite gorgeous. The flower is known for its use in leis and other jewelry that Hawaiians wear, and it is just all around a good flower.

The hibiscus flower is known to attract love and lust to those who wear it or its scent. If you are looking for a powerful love spell, this is the one to attract your one true love. Be careful, though, if not done correctly, you will only attract a lot of lustful lovers, and if that is not what you are looking for, it can make it harder to find your true love.

If you are into divination, this plant will also help you, as it can help open your third eye to the future. You need only to trust it. It will also help with dreams like the dandelion. Try combining them for some powerful visions in your dreams.

Lavender

This purple flower is very important in a witch's stock. It has several uses, but most of them all have to do with its soothing aroma. Admit it, lavender anything smells pretty nice, as long as they use pure lavender oil, and not a synthetic lavender scent that is headache inducing, sickly sweet, and honestly makes it smell like you have a gas leak in your house.

Lavender is a purifying herb. This means it's used to banish any bad things that are in your house, life, or anywhere else. It is like the cleaning agent of the herb world. It will cleanse you from head to toe and leave you feeling fresh as if you had just taken a shower.

It is also used for giving you sweet dreams. It does not give you prophecies, rather, it lets you sleep easy, and not be interrupted by bad dreams so that you can wake up with a good outlook on life and you can wake up feeling rested. There are bath lotions out there for adults and babies alike that are for this exact purpose. You use them before you go to bed right after your bath or shower, and you will sleep easy. It is encouraged for parents to give their babies a bath in this every night before bed to help them establish a sleep pattern.

It also brings happiness and love. Not from others but yourself. Lavender is a great addition to a self-love potion or spell, as it will open your mind to spiritual growth and allow you to see the beauty in yourself, and you will become a happier and more loving person.

Lavender is a great herb to keep with you pretty much at all times in a little emergency herb bag. You can use it whenever you need it.

Mugwort

This is a very spiritual herb. It is used to open the doors to your inner soul. If you are scared to see the depth of your truest self, don't use too much of this herb.

It enhances the moons psychic receptive qualities and allows you to be more in tune with the world around you as well as with yourself. You can use this if you want to open your eyes to the things around you and see things for what they truly are.

Nutmeg

This is not just a topping for your hot cocoa or eggnog. This is actually a very useful herb in the Wiccan culture.

It is a great relaxation tool and can be used to ease stresses. That is why it is often used in such calming relaxing drinks. It also invites happiness into your life. So if you want to be stress-free and happy, this is the herb for you.

Rosemary

This is a very useful herb in the kitchen and our lives. Most people only see rosemary as a herb to brine a turkey in, or to brighten up a plate, but it is so much more than that.

This herb gives you clarity. It helps you see the world for what it truly is. Mixed with mugwort, it can be a powerful combination. You will see the world clearly for possibly the first time if you use these in a clarity spell.

It will also give you inner peace, so if you have something that is bugging you, and you just can't seem to let it go, then you should put some rosemary in tea, and drink it. It will help you find your inner clarity.

Sage

Sage has many uses, and a lot of times it depends on the type of sage that you are using. I know a lot of people think sage is sage, but there is sage that is almost white, sage that is more purple, there is even really dark green type of sage. Sage comes in a variety of colors and has a variety of uses.

It can bring about inner peace, and wisdom to boot. Inner peace is what we all strive for, and if it is mixed with rosemary, you will find yourself calm and collected so that you can gather the wisdom that you need without an inner battle raging on inside your head.

It can also aid fertility, healing, and help you lead a long and happy life. If that sentence right there is not enough for you to put sage on everything in your life, I don't know what is. Sage is the master of life, death, and everything in between it seems.

Sage can also be used for cleansing, purification, and protection. I mean, is there anything it can't do? Other than making your crush fall in love with you, I don't believe there is anything else that it can't do.

Thyme

This is the butt of many people's holiday jokes due to how the name is pronounced. However, this branch like herb is not just for jokes. It can improve longevity in your life, and make you stronger and have more energy. With the energy to get stuff done, and the life left to do it in, you may find you have a little extra thyme on your hands (sorry, couldn't resist).

It's a great confidence booster. It can help you get the courage to talk to the guy or girl that you are crushing on, or give you the courage to go for that big promotion. This is just all around a great herb to have in your stock.

Practical and Magical Tips for Working with Herbs

There are many things that you should remember when you are going to be working with herbs, as well as when you're purchasing them. Herbs only work when they are in the right conditions, and if they have been picked at the right time, or planted, at the right time.

Herbs are great in spells, but they are tricky, and they work best under the right conditions.

Purchasing Herbs

When you are purchasing herbs already planted and picked, make sure that you are buying whole herbs, and from a place that caters to witches and the Wiccan religion (if possible) to ensure that they are planted and picked at the right time. You also don't want to buy pre-crushed herbs, because some spells call for you to crush them a certain way, and some spells call for the herb to be intact, and if this is the case, that means that you would then have to buy an intact herb to add to your collection. It is a lot easier to buy them whole and crush them yourself.

Also, when purchasing herbs, make sure that you purchase most of them dry if you are just doing it for storage. If you have a ritual in a day or two that requires fresh herbs and you are already at the shop, then go ahead and buy fresh, but for most rituals, you only need dried herbs.

If you are purchasing online, only go through a trusted Wiccan provider. Otherwise, you may not get what you think you were supposed to be getting. You could get herbs that were picked at the wrong time or planted just a little too late. You want ones that are just right.

Creating Your Own Herb Garden

The best way to avoid being bamboozled with herbs that were not carefully cultivated is to create your own magical garden, and filling it with the herbs of your choice. Be careful, though, because herbs can be very finicky plants to grow, and you may have to try a few times before you have any success even getting them to grow, let alone getting them to grow well enough to use in your spells.

When you are planting your garden, you should take into consideration all of the things that go into growing a garden, and then the magical aspects of growing your own magical herb garden. Things such as astrology, moon cycles, timing, and much more.

Once you have got it all down, you'll find that you are saving money by growing your own herbs, and it is nice to always have a supply on hand when you need them.

Astrology and the Elements in Gardening

Unlike with normal gardening, the elements and astrology have a lot to do with herbal gardening, because they are what infuse the herbs with their magical properties. Just like humans have astrological signs, so do plants. And some are best planted at different times and picked at different times. You must learn when to plant a certain plant to gain the most magic out of them.

Some plants only grow the best, hence with the most magic, if planted during the right moon cycle. So you have to pay close attention to when that is as well. While it takes a lot of work, you will be sure to get the most magic out of your plants if you plant them at the right times according to what they need.

Gathering in the Wild

Of course, you can always gather in the wild. This ensures that they grew at the right time, and if you get there at the right time, you can pick them at the perfect moment, and they will definitely be ready. Nature makes no mistakes.

However, the surplus of a lot of herbs in the wild is lessening more and more as deforestation takes place.

There is also no guarantee that you will find any herbs that you're looking for if you don't live in an area where the herbs are commonly grown. However, it is always fun to go out searching for just the right dandelion or just the right daffodil.

Drying and Storing Herbs

It's important that if you pick fresh herbs, you dry them right away unless you just picked them for a ritual you are doing that night that requires fresh herbs.

To do this lay the herbs out flat on a piece of paper and cover them with another piece of paper. Leave them like this for ten days, changing the paper daily. Then you should store them in a cool, dry, dark place to keep from charging them with the wrong energy.

Section 3

An Herbal Grimoire

Getting Started with Herbal Magic

Now that you know what you need to know about herbs, let us move on to a bit of herbal magic, shall we?

In this section, we'll talk about a few herb spells to add to your book of shadows.

Magical Teas

There are several teas out there that we drink every day. Wouldn't it be great if they had a purpose? Well, now they can have just that. With this little section here, you will learn that tea can be of great use to you in your life, and can even have magical properties if it is brewed with the right herbs.

But first, let us ask ourselves, what is tea? Is it a bunch of specified leaves, or can any type of herb be made into a tea? The answer is the latter. As long as it is edible, it can be used in a tea. Cinnamon is a little harder to make into a tea, but not impossible. You just have to grind it up really fine.

You can make a tea out of rosemary and thyme. It would taste a little bit odd as a drink, but it is very possible, and actually a lot of Wiccans use those two in their teas due to their ability to open the mind and help you find inner peace.

Magical Evening Tea

Such as the magical evening tea. This tea helps you relax and sleep. It has several herbs in it, so you have to make your own tea bags.

What you need

Nutmeg

Valerian root

Rosemary

Chamomile

Dandelion

Tea Bag of Coffee Filter

Hot Water

Put all of the ingredients in a tea bag or wrap them in a coffee filter and bind with twine. Fill your cup up with hot water and allow your tea to steep for five minutes before drinking.

Divination Tea

This tea will help unlock your third eye to help you with your divination skills.

What you need

- Chamomile

- Dandelion

- Hibiscus

- Tea Bag or Coffee Filter

- Hot water

As before, put all of the ingredients into a tea bag and steep for five minutes before drinking. Before taking the first sip say this chant:

Goddess give me the visions

Open my eye to see

Produce the answers of the world

and show them to me

Then you can go about drinking your tea.

Magical Baths

There are many magical baths out there such as ones to help find love. A few were mentioned in my book *Wicca: Book of Shadows*, in the love section.

Magical baths are literally baths that you take with a specified blend of herbs and candles to achieve the effect that you want in your life. These baths can be for healing, for love, to help draw in money, and a whole plethora of other things that you wish to accomplish in your life. When using these baths, keep in mind that you're going to be soaking until the water is no longer warm. Having the heater on if it's winter time may be a good idea. These baths require you to stay in there until the water gets cold, or forty-five minutes, whichever comes first. The longer you can soak in these baths, the better.

If you do not have a giant fancy soaking tub, no problem, use the tub you have. If you do not have a bathtub, a horse basin will suffice, just heat up the water on the stove, and pour it in the basin, and you will have your water for a bath. These baths are not for washing, so do not use soap with these baths. You take a regular bath or shower afterward.

There is no certain setup that you have to use when you are taking these baths. Some of them do require candles, while others don't. If the bath doesn't require candles, that does not mean that you absolutely have to do it with no candles. You can add candles just to set a relaxing mood if you so desire. You can add other herbs such as rose petals, or chamomile if you so desire to get that truly relaxed vibe.

The point of these baths is to relax, and let the herbs seep into you and do their job. You have to be able to relax when taking a magical bath, so make sure that you do it at a time when you can have some privacy. If you have kids, plan accordingly. It is very important that you have peace, quiet, and privacy when you take these baths, as any disruption of energy can cause them not to work properly. You have to keep the energy flowing smoothly the entire time, and having your significant other, kids, or any other person popping in to ask a question will disrupt the flow.

Once you have established a good place and time to do your baths, you can start planning which bath you want to use.

Clear Psychic Channel Bath

This bath is to help you clear your mind, and open your third eye to the world around you. You want to take this bath when you are clear-minded, so leave all of your stresses and worries outside of the bathroom door when you go to do this.

What You Need

Basil

Bay

Dandelion leaves

Mugwort leaves

Fill the tub halfway, and then add the leaves in before filling the tub all the way. This allows the leaves to steep properly and distribute throughout the water evenly. Make sure that you are calm and open when you step in the bath. Imagine that your mind has a door and that this door is opening as you soak and relax in the bath. If you feel that you are getting too tense, then say the chant, *I am open to the world, send me your visions*. Once you have soaked, allowed the bath to work its magic, then you can get out of the bath, clean your tub, and take your regular bath or shower.

** Note** Make sure that you have a good hair trap, or screen in your tub to catch the herbs when you drain your tub. Dry herbs will expand and clump and may cause severe plumbing problems. To avoid this, simply get a hair trap, and you will be clear.

Good Vibrations Spell

This spell will help bring good vibes into your life and to help you have a good week and keep on track. This bath welcomes good luck and prosperity into your life as well.

What You Need

- Chamomile

- Rose Petals

- Cinnamon

- Blessed Thistle

Fill the bath up half way and add the chamomile, cinnamon, and blessed thistle. Let the bath fill up, and then add the rose petals to the water, and around the rim of the tub. It will look like the scene from a romance novel.

An Intro to Herb and Candle Magic

Some spells require the combined use of both herbs and candles for them to work. These spells are generally regarded as strong spells, though a lot of them are easy to perform.

Similar to ritual baths, find a place to do these spells that will give you peace and quiet. Magic is about continuous, uninterrupted energy, and if someone interrupts that energy, the spell will not work, or it will go horribly wrong. So make sure that you find a place that is quiet and peaceful, even if it means finding an abandoned cabin on the outskirts of your town to do you spells in.

As for the spells that you can do with candles and herbs, the options are nearly limitless. You can do love spells, prosperity spells and spells to promote happiness. If you are unfamiliar with candle magic, there will be more about it in the fourth book of this series, *Wicca: Candle Magic*. However, here are two spells to get you started.

Healing Love Spell

This spell will help you fix a romance that may need a little help. If you use this spell, then you can boost a relationship that you are in, or help heal your love for yourself. This little spell is a dandy to have on hand. If you want to be a great witch, this spell, or one like it, should probably make its way into your book of shadows.

What You need

- ⅄ Lavender Oil

- ⅄ dried blueberries

- ⅄ Tamarind

- Mint

- Sea Salt

- Jasmine Incense

- 4 White Candles

- Rain Water

- Dirt

- Cauldron

- Matches

- Sheet of Paper

- Charcoal

Light the white candles as you cast your circle. One candle for each of the cardinal directions. Then put the cauldron in the center of the circle. Using the candle that represents north, light the jasmine incense.

Write the name of the person(s) you want to heal, and then put three drops of lavender oil on the paper. You should write the names in charcoal. Throw the paper pieces in the cauldron and then add tamarind, dried blueberries, mint, and salt on top of the paper. Take each candle starting with the west, and drop three drops of wax onto the mixture in the cauldron. Burn the contents that are in the cauldron. Once it has burned down, then you burn the ashes. Add the rain water and the dirt, mix it with the ashes and pour the contents into a pouch or envelope. Then bury it that same night.

Money Attraction Spell

This spell will help you bring money into your life. If you are finding yourself struggling financially, then you should definitely give this a try. It will not make you rich, but it will bring some extra change to your life. You may find yourself finding more change here and there.

What You Need

- ⚲ Allspice Incense

- ⚲ Three Green Candles

- ⚲ Money Attracting Oil

Place the Candles in a triangle, and cast your circle. Anoint the candles with the oil, and then light them. Use the candles to light the incense. Sit in the circle, and imagine yourself raking in gallons of coins and bills. Sit like this until the candles burn down, then close your circle, blow out the incense and watch the money start to roll in.

Magical Oils

There are also a lot of oils made from herbs, and they are not hard to find. Look for stores that sell essential oils, and make sure that they are one hundred percent natural. These oils are blended carefully with a specific purpose in mind. Nowadays you can buy some already made at the store. However, they tend to not have the same effect as ones that you create yourself. The reason is that they were made with someone else's intentions, and they will work more for the creator's purposes than for you.

There are several ways that you can use these oils. However, you use them, make sure that you are using the right ones to get the right outcome. To use them, you can do as follows.

- ⚔ **Anoint your body**: To do this, take the oil, and rub it onto your skin. You want to make sure that you are rubbing it in in the direction that you want the magic to work. Towards your head, if you want the magic to work towards you, and towards your feet, if you want it to work away from you.

- ⚔ **Anoint a magical piece**: This can be a candle or a bracelet or whatever you are using for the spell. Again rub the oil in the way that you want the magic to go.

- ❁ **Diffuser**: Whenever you want the effects of the oils, you can put them into a diffuser that spreads the oil out over the general area in a vapor. These are great if you are stressed and don't have the privacy for a spell. Just pour the oil in the diffuser and let the magic do the work.

Magical oils are an important part of many spells, and it's good to know how to create your own.

Making the Oil

What You Need

- ❁ Carrier Oil

- ❁ Herbs for your oil

- ❁ Mortar and Pestle

- ❁ Storage vials and containers

Take roughly two ounces of carrier oil for two tablespoons of the herbs and put them in your mortar. Crush the herbs into the oil, and really get them in there. Pour the mixture into a bottle and cap it tightly. Store for three days in a dark consecrated room. After the three days you can add more herbs if necessary, but if the oil is potent enough, strain it through a cheesecloth, and then store in a dark bottle with a benzoin tincture for preservation.

A note on carrier oil. It has to be neutral. Not in smell per se, but in its energy. Carrier oils are oils that will distribute the scent and energy of the herbs evenly. You want to choose the right one for the job. Also if you are buying pure essential oils, and are just adding herbs to those to make your own special oil, then you are going to need a base. Essential oils are generally too strong to apply directly on the body. For more information on essential oils and base oils, visit http://blessedbe.sugarbane.com/oils.htm to learn what each oil is best used for.

In the fashion of the rest of this book, here are a few examples of how to make your own essential oils for various reasons, and spells. Remember when you are making the oils to keep your mind on the task at hand and the purpose of the oils, otherwise, they will not work very well.

Prosperity Oil

This oil is used to bring you luck and good fortune. This oil is very fluid. You can rub it on yourself, a good luck charm, or anoint a candle with it.

What You Need

- ⚐ Heather oil

- ⚐ Frankincense oil

- ⚲ Cinnamon oil

- ⚲ Mineral Oil

- ⚲ Blessed thistle

- ⚲ Tincture

To make this oil, first mix the blessed thistle with the heather, frankincense, and cinnamon oils. Bottle and cap tightly, let set for four days. Strain and add the mineral oil and tincture before pouring into a dark colored bottle and storing.

To use this oil, anoint it wherever it is needed. A good tip is to anoint your wallet or purse with this so that you will never be without money. You can also use it to anoint a candle before doing a money attraction spell, or a prosperity spell.

Love Attraction Oil

While you cannot force a person to fall in love with you, you can attract love to you. This oil helps you do that. You want one that is strong, but not too strong. Otherwise you will also attract a bunch of people who are just wanting a fling. So you want more of a subtle attractant than an all out aphrodisiac.

What You Need

- ↟ Apricot Oil

- ↟ Chamomile

- ↟ Coconut Oil

To make this oil, crush the chamomile into the apricot oil, pour into a bottle, cap, and let sit for three days. Once you do this, check to see if the chamomile had seeped into the apricot oil enough. If not, let sit two more days before straining and bottling with the coconut oil and tincture.

To use this oil, anoint yourself with it on your neck and wrists almost as if you are using perfume. You can also anoint a candle with it in a love spell. There are a few of these oils in *Wicca: Book of Shadows*.

Oils can help your everyday spells, but do not rely too heavily on them. Every witch has a style, but as a beginner, it is best to get in as much variety as you can to ensure that you are truly engulfed in educating yourself in the ways of Wicca.

Other Magical Creations

Most of these are known as lucky charms and talismans that hold magic and disperse the magic when needed. Dream catchers are an example of a magical creation. They are made to catch nightmares, often woven with turquoise to ward off evil spirits and bad dreams.

Magical creations can be ordinary objects that you have used in a ritual and infused with magic. You could have a blanket that you rubbed with lavender and said a peace spell over to help encourage a good night's sleep. Your purse can be rubbed with money attraction oil to help you draw in more money. There are a few things that are made for magic.

These magical creations are things such as witch bottles and sachets. They are made specifically for the person who creates them, so it is best to make them yourself. Otherwise you will not have the best outcome. You may get it to work a little, but for the best results, it is better to do one yourself. They are easy to make and do not require a high magic level.

Here are a couple of magical items that you can make right now. These are simple things won't take a lot of time to make.

Lucky Charm Sachet

A sachet is a little bag that is sewn together with a magic spell inside. The purpose of these is to carry the magic with you wherever you go or to hang them up to use the magic in a specific area. They are small and inconspicuous, but they work pretty well. You need bags with certain colors. Little drawstring pouches work best.

What You Need

- A small piece of cloth/drawstring pouch

- Acorn

- hammer (can be a miniature replica)

- tigers eye stone

- Piece of paper

- pen

Write what you want to achieve on the piece of paper, fold it up, and place it in the bag. Place the hammer, acorn, and tiger's eye stone on top of the paper, and close up the bag. Hold it in your hand and say this chant.

Bag of Magic powers

Bring me luck and prosperity

God of Creation and Goddess High

unleash the magic that is inside

Place the bag where you need it, or carry it with you wherever you go. The choice is yours. You want to put it where it is most. Also, make sure that you do not lose it. It won't benefit anyone else, but losing it means that you have to make a new one, and even though it isn't hard, it can be inconvenient.

Prophetic Dream Pillow

Dream pillows are another magical item that are good to know how to make. They open your mind to divination and help you remember what you dreamt about if you have a prophetic dream. These pillows are used by those who want to have stronger connections with the spirit world to have stronger visions.

You can buy dream pillows commercially, or you can make your own. The way you make them is up to you, and you can fill them with as many or as few herbs as you would like. However, make sure to balance your intent. You do not want too much of one herb, and not enough of another. Otherwise, your prophetic dreams will be skewed

Here are some things that you can put into your pillow. These herbs will help open your mind and help you relax enough to sleep.

⅄ **Alecost**: This promotes your contact with the

Goddess.

- ⅄ **Angelica**: Allows your inner eye to open for prophetic dreams and visions along with protection from evil forces while you sleep.

- ⅄ **Bay Laurel**: This gives you creative inspiration and spiritual protection while also stimulating your third eye.

- ⅄ **Bee Balm**: This should be included in all of your pillows. It promotes a restful sleep so that you are not tired after a night of prophetic dreams.

- ⅄ **Black Mustard Seeds**: These repel demons of the night and other evil forces.

- ⅄ **Calendula Blossoms**: Gives you a restful nights sleep.

- ⅄ **Catnip**: For romantic dreams and sound sleep. However, if you have cats, they may steal your pillow.

- ⅄ **Chamomile**: This provides financially inspirational dreams.

- ⅄ **Cloves**: Promotes restful sleep along with erotic and psychic dreams.

- ⚼ **Henna**: Good fortune, and psychic grounding.

- ⚼ **Hops**: Not just for beer anymore. Hops promote deep sleep and healing.

- ⚼ **Lavender Blossoms:** Peaceful, sweet dreams and communication with the spirit world.

There are many different herbs that you can put in your pillow, and what is listed is just the beginning. You can also make your pillow as big or as small as you would like, and you can make it as fancy or as simple as you please.

Smudging Rituals

Smudging is the act of burning herbs in an area to create a magical barrier. It is generally used to purify a room or clear it of negative energy. It is a common native American ritual, and it has since passed to the Wiccan religion, which has adapted the rituals to include all different types of spells. You can even do a smudge for a love spell with Wiccan traditions.

Earlier, we covered how to make a smudge stick. You literally only have to tie the herbs up and dry them. Once they are dry, trim them up so that they are even. Once you do that, you can burn the smudge stick. Make several to keep on hand for whatever purposes you may need them to serve.

There are many different spells that you can use these rituals for, and the spells vary from genre to genre. Here are a few that are easy to do.

Clearing Unwanted Energy

This spell is good for use if you have an unwanted energy or presence in your household. It is simple, and it doesn't require many ingredients.

What You Need

- White sage smudge stick

- White Candle

- Fireproof bowl

- Matches

Clear everyone out of the house but yourself. Cast your circle. After you have opened the spell, light the candle, and ask the Goddess to be with you in your spell. Use the candle to light the smudge stick, and then place it in the bowl. Move throughout each room, wafting the smoke in every corner, and say this prayer in every room as well.

Goddess of the Moon and sky

clear this house and make it shine

All evil be banished from inside

as I say, my will be thine!

Once you have cleansed every room, including attic and crawlspace/basement if possible, then you can put out your smudge stick, and dispose of it properly.

Enhancing Communications with Plants

Plants have spirits just like we do. The only difference is that plants do not have mouths from which they can speak and verbally be heard. However, we can still communicate with them in some ways. Talking to them helps them grow, as we are giving them extra carbon monoxide and heat, but they also feel our energies and the love we have for them.

To connect with a plant and know how it feels can be a little tricky. The hardest part is not feeling silly when you go about doing it. You must believe that it will work, even if it doesn't work at first. So to get out of your head, first, do some meditating. As you meditate, imagine yourself being a plant. That usually helps you get over the awkwardness of trying to talk to a plant telepathically.

After you have meditated, choose a plant that you want to talk to. Trees are generally the easiest to start with as they are big and full of energy. Place your palm on the tree and close your eyes. Imagine your energy is a green ball. Picture that green ball going into the tree, and melding with the tree's green ball of energy. If you have done it successfully, you will begin to feel what the tree is feeling. Choose an old sacred tree if you want to really know if you are connecting and can feel the tree's feelings. You will be able to feel the pain of the tree almost as if it were your own.

Don't get discouraged if you cannot get it on the first try. It takes some time and a lot of practice. Best of luck.

Wicca

Candle Magic

A Beginner's Guide to Mastering Wiccan Candle Magic with Candle Spells

Valerie W. Holt

Section 1

The Wonder of Fire

Our Connection with Fire

Were you ever called a pyro in school, or made fun of for
your love of fire? The truth is that you're not the only fire
lover in this world. Fire is a big part of the Wiccan culture
because it is one of the elements. We are so connected with
fire because it is a part of nature. Just as we are connected
with the earth, we may be even more connected with fire,
because it is such an essential part of our lives and our
spells.

Fire dances across the wilderness as if nothing blocks its
path. It is dangerous, and it is beautiful at the same time,
and if that doesn't leave you with terrified awe, I don't
know what will. Because fire is one of the most
mesmerizing wonders of nature, our ability to connect with
it is astounding.

Why do we connect with fire so well? Perhaps, because like
us, it is entirely misunderstood, or pushed aside as
unimportant. Or, perhaps because it is such an essential
part of a lot of spells. We spend much time with it during
spells that we've created a bond with it. There are multiple

theories why we connect with fire, and no single one is correct. The bottom line is that it is an essential part of many Wiccan rituals, and that is why candles are used.

Candles in Wiccan Rituals

Candles are often used in many spells, but they are used even more so in ritual spells. A true ritual spell will have you open your circle with a candle that represents each element, and probably a white one as well for purification.

Candles are part of a Wiccan's necessary items to complete a majority of spells. They are always there and are never a waste. Even when they are not needed, some Wiccans prefer to open their circles with candles every time, rather than just open their circles by calling the elements, and that is perfectly okay. If you have the time, then there is no harm in setting up the candles every time.

If you have come this far in the Wicca series, and you do not see the importance of candles yet, then this book will change your mind. Being the fourth book in this series, you have already read about some spells that involve candles, but there are more rituals that are based on candles alone. Most people think of herbs when they think of Wicca spells and magic, but the truth is that candles are just as powerful if they are used correctly.

Wiccans often use candles to bring them prosperity or protection, or any number of other reasons that they need to perform a spell. Sometimes they use candles to light smudge sticks because candles have the steadiest flames.

Candles offer natural light right at your fingertips and can be used to find the things you need. You could even do a protection spell with the same candle you are using for light. Candles also heat things up, such as herbs when you need to have the herbs warmed so that they are primed and ready to be used. There are few limitations with candles.

Fire Magic

Fire magic is the magic we make using fire itself, rather than the color of a candle. This magic calls upon the element fire. An example of a fire spell is a warming spell when we are out in the cold. Fire magic is remarkable because you can feel the warmth of fire when you are nowhere near an open flame.

To use fire magic, you must be open to handling an element without a circle. This can get very out of control and takes a lot of practice. However, if you are prepared to do it, you will find that there are some amazing things that you can do.

There are a lot of Wiccans that doubt you can really harness the power of the elements, and it is true to an extent from what I have seen. Example, you cannot start a fire without a spark, but once you get a little ember, you can call fire to you to emblazon that ember and keep it burning for a good while.

You can also call fire to you to help you get that pesky pilot light on your heater lit. Fire has also been called upon by witches, to protect you from harm. There are many spells for harnessing the raw power of fire that it is a little scary. If everyone were to try them at once, it could get a little out of control with how unpredictable fire can be.

The Role of Color

Color plays an important role with candle magic. If you get the wrong colored candle and try to do a spell, then you may end up with a completely different result. You could be trying to get more money, but if you choose a blue candle, then you may wake up with longer hair—you never know. Colors are important; there are only five colors of candles in Wiccan tradition. Black and Grey are for darker magic, and none of them will be covered in this book. You will also use subsets of colors, such as pink and orange. While Green and Purple are considered secondary or subset colors as well, each of those is a primary in Wicca because of their representation of an element.

Blue

Blue candles can increase wisdom. You use these when you want to know more about the world, and you want to open your mind to receiving information you would otherwise be closed off to. Blue candles can also bring happiness, and bring you prosperity when combined with a green candle. There are many other uses for this candle as well, such as helping you deal with stressful situations.

Green

Green candles are the money candles. It brings wealth and prosperity to you. If you are looking to make more money, there are a million spells out there, and I bet that ninety percent of them involve you using a green candle in some way or another. It also helps with healing. Just as it can help heal your broken finances, it can also help with healing your ailments. It can bring more love into your life, and banish immorality. Green is the symbol of hope, of a new beginning.

Yellow

Yellow candles are known as "pick me up" candles. What do you think of when you think of the color yellow? You think sunshine and daffodils and daisies and so many other bright and happy things, right? Yellow is great for warding off depression or bringing a depressed person out of an almost catatonic depressed state. Yellow candles can also add happiness and energy into a room. Yellow is great for sharpening the mind and perpetuating kindness and bringing in new friendships.

Red

This is the color of passion. Of strength. Of courage. This is the color you see when you are so angry that you could scream, and also the color you feel when you are so into someone that you feel your heart is going to explode. Red brings energy into a room. It brings motivation as well. Red candles are used in a lot of motivation spells because of the energy courage and strength that it brings.

Pink

This candle is for love spells—almost exclusively. Pink is for attracting love. Not only from others but yourself. It is for personal success as well. It can bring you the success you need in many different endeavors, whether they be business or love related.

Orange

The combination of yellow and red, it is a mixture of passion and happiness. It makes sense that this color would be perfect for healing broken relationships and mending

162

friendships. It is also great when paired with a yellow candle to bring happiness into the room.

Purple

This is the color of clairvoyance. The color of divination. The color of magic itself. This color represents Spirit, the guiding light and the place where our magic comes from. This color can relieve the emotional pain that has built up over the years and can be a great calming color. Use it for meditation. It will bring you inner peace so you can concentrate. Not to mention it is a beautiful color all around due to the many different hues that it comes in, no two of them are even remotely similar.

White

White candles are for protection, purification, and healing. You should have a white candle lit any time you are doing a sort of blood letting in a ritual. You are literally giving your DNA to whatever takes up your blood as an offering, and without a white candle, or purification, your blood could be offered to an evil spirit. Lighting a white candle is how you protect yourself. It creates a shield to keep the unwanted spirits away.

Color plays a major role in magic. Each color has an attribute, and each attribute is unique. Pick the right color to get the right result. Pick a color to focus your energy on because it is not just about color, it is about the energy that is associated with it, and how strongly your energy is connected to the candle's energy.

Stay connected to the basis of what you want the spell to do, and if you are trying to send your energy out to every candle, then you will have some problems because your energy will not be as strong as it would be if you were just focusing on one candle. The only exception is in a ritual where you must have the five elements and the white candle burning, or if you have to combine two candles for a certain spell to make it more powerful. If your spell only requires one candle color, then follow the spell. Always make sure that you have the right color.

Section 2

Preparing for Candle Magic

Candles for Spell Work

There are different types of candles that you can use to
burn. However, there are only a few types that work well in
the witch community. Feel free to use any kind if you do
not need to mark it with symbols or charge it. (i.e. lower
level spell) But, once you get into higher level candle magic
you are going to need certain types of candles.

There are big and small tea light candles; there are small
and medium glass encased candles, there are big and small
chub candles and taper candles. Your options are so vast
that it can get confusing after awhile, so this section will be
a guide to help you figure out what candles you need to
make your spells easier and most effective.

Big Chub Candles

Big chub candles are the ones that you would generally put
in a cute glass dish. They are kind of fat and either flat on
top or sort of tapered. It all depends on who makes them.
These are great when you need the flame to last a while,
and when you need to carve a symbol into it, as it has a
good surface area to carve a symbol clearly, and you don't
have to worry about it being too obscure to be effective.

Small Chub Candles

These are great for when you need it to burn down quickly but still have to carve a symbol in your candle. Their burn time is a lot shorter than a big chub so if you must burn a candle all the way down in one shot, and don't have a lot of time, this is the way to go.

Big Taper

If you have ever seen a menorah, then you know what a taper candle looks like. These candles are long, skinny, and get thinner as they go up. These are great if you do not have to carve a symbol. They burn easily and are very elegant, even more so than chub candles, as the have a very sleek look to them. If you have time to let them burn down, or you can use them for more than one ritual, then these are the ones to go for on spells that do not require a symbol carving.

Small Taper

These are a little harder to find if it is not close to the holiday season, so make sure to stock up. These small, sleek candles are good for witch bottles because you have to let the candle burn out, so you already want a small candle. An alternative is bottle corks, but they're notoriously small, and a chub would not really work for a witch bottle. Since you don't need a symbol on your candle, a small taper is perfect for these.

Tea Light Candles

These candles are good for calling the elements, especially if you can find colored ones. They burn for a short amount of time, but long enough for you to do a spell, and if the ritual takes hours, there are big tea lights. Stock up on the colored ones in the spring in most areas, because that is when the colored ones seem to be out with any semblance of regularity.

Glass Encased Candles

These should not be used in a Wiccan ritual. They are for home decoration only, and the scents that are often infused in them are not natural and can throw off the balance of your spell. You want nothing but natural candles in your spells so that the energy can be balanced.

Choosing a Candle

Using the previous subsection as a reference, it should be easier to make a decision for what candle you need when it comes to shapes and color. However, there are much more considerations to choosing a candle. Think of where you are going to be doing the ritual. What type of candle holders do you have at your disposal? How easy is wax cleanup? Have the right candle so you can focus your energy on the candle itself, and not worry about messes or fire or any other hazard that may arise.

If you are in a dry area, it is best to have a bucket of water on hand to extinguish a fire in case a candle falls over and catches something on fire. You want to have everything ready in case of emergency so that you can breathe easy when you light the candle and begin the spell.

Pay attention to how a candle is manufactured. If it is not manufactured using natural ingredients, then you shouldn't use it because Wicca is about being as natural as possible. You want candles that are made from soy wax, not paraffin wax. Paraffin wax can be used in a pinch, but it can cause some imbalance issues with the spell.

You should also pick up the candles yourself, rather than order them online because you want to find candles that mesh with your energies. Inanimate objects might seem like a weird thing to mesh with, but trust me, just like with your book of shadows, you want to be compatible with the candles that you buy. Find a brand and stick with that brand because they are generally all manufactured the same way.

Being Practical

Use your candles with practical intentions. You cannot buy a candle and expect your spell to be the power of a level ten expert. You must put in the practice.

A lot of people give up on magic because they do not think it works for them. They want riches with a money spell, so they don't even notice the random change that they are finding just laying around. Instead, they want to find a duffel bag stuffed with money. This is an example of how not to be practical. If you are using a wealth spell, pay attention to the pennies that you find, and the weird places that they keep popping up. Think about where you picked up that dime. Be patient, and practical with your magic. Otherwise, you will end up giving up on candle magic.

Consecrating Your Candles

Prepare your candles, and purify them before you use them. While some spells may need less of an in-depth consecration of candles than other spells, it is best to know the basis of the spell before you try.

Clearing

You must clear all your candles. Before you even put them in storage, you should clear your candles. To do this, wash them in warm water and say a clearing spell over them such as

Power of water

wash this candle

make it a blank slate

Simple chant, no rhyme, but it clears the candle of all residue that may taint it from the outside world.

Clearing allows your candles to become pure again, no matter what contaminants they have touched in processing and handling, or even just sitting on the shelves in the store. You want clear candles that have no association with everything, almost like a blank slate. This allows you to have the best energy flow from your candle and is important in your endeavors as a new witch.

Charging

Not all spells require a charged candle, though it is good to practice to have some handy. If you have a spell like a witch bottle, you do not need a charged candle, as it is fire mixed with color that does the magic along with what is inside the bottle. For spells that rely on just candle magic, then you must charge your candle. To do that you have to first make sure that it is clear.

Then you wait for a new moon. The new moon symbolizes a fresh beginning, and that is what you want for your candles. Unlike with crystals, where you want a full moon, you want the new moon to charge your candle like a blank slate so that it is ready for whatever spell that you need.

Just before you lay your candles in a window, or outside, say a spell over them to open them up to being charged. You can use one such as

Vessel of fire

take in the night

let it charge you

and make you bright

It doesn't have to be intricate; it just has to open the candle up to the new moon cycle. Certain spells may call for you to charge your candle at a different moon phase but the process is still the same. Open it up to charging and leave it in the view of the moon.

Anointing

A lot of spells call for you to anoint your candle with an oil of some sort that relates to the spell. These can be oils such as good luck oils, or protection oils.

When you anoint the candle make sure that you rub the oil into the candle, don't just pour it on the candle. Rub the oil in the direction you want the magic to go. If you want the magic to come to you, then rub the oil into the candle starting from the side farthest from you, and work your way in. If you want the magic to go out into the world, then start at the candle side closest to you and work your way out.

Anointing is done quite often, but not in all spells. Be prepared to use it often.

Carving Symbols

Some spells, generally higher level spells, require you to carve symbols into your candles. These symbols are to stabilize the flow of energy to stop a disaster from happening, or to stop the wrong entity from answering the call of your spell. A lot of higher level spells have a wider broadcasting range rather than a direct line to the Goddess herself, and there is a lot of evil out there that can answer the call. Symbols help you keep the direct line to the Goddess, rather than sending out a free-range signal that will invite evil. If you have to carve a symbol in your candle, then you should light a white candle just in case to keep yourself safe. Better safe than sorry.

If you are carving a symbol into your candle, using a clean, sharp knife blade works best (although anything sharp can work). You want whatever you are using to be clean like an X-ACTO knife blade which will give you precision cuts so that you do not have any mistakes that make you have to try again. Also, before you mess up a candle, you should practice cutting the design out on a scrap chunk of wax. You can make these scrap blocks by melting down the stubs of old candles and pouring them into a square mold. Once you are good at cutting the design into wax, then you can move onto the candle, this way you are not wasting candles.

Timing

When consecrating your candles, remember that some spells can only be done at a certain period of time. Make sure that you do not neglect the time period as such neglect can turn a great spell into a dud. In the magic world, time in hours is irrelevant, time in moon cycles is very important, and if you do not pay attention to the moon cycle, you can have some major problems.

Section 3

Candle Magic and Spells

Getting Started

To get started, you must first be sure that you have an array of candles ready at your disposal, because, without candles, these spells will not work. Make sure that you have all the colors you need, in all the sizes and shapes required. A Wiccan's storeroom typically looks like a candle shop threw up in it. If money is tight, stock up a bit at a time until you are ready to do your spellwork.

You can also make your own candles if it proves to be more cost-effective. If you want to turn an area of your home into a candle making center, then, by all means, bypass commercial businesses and get as close to nature as you can. It is encouraged in the Wiccan community.

Also, make sure that you have what you need to consecrate your candles. Materials such as oils and the tools to carve symbols when you get to that point. You want to be able just to grab and go whenever you need a spell, not run around trying to find the stuff you need.

Once you are prepared for a candle apocalypse, it is time to try some small spells using candle magic.

Love Spells

Love spells are tricky because people often feel that they can make someone fall in love with them even if they don't want to. You can't do that. Be careful with your intentions on a love spell. The most you can do is make someone overly infatuated with you, and when the spell wears off, it can go either one of two ways. They come to their senses and treat you like an outcast for breaking basic morality rules, or they can become dangerously obsessed with you, to the point they could kill you if they thought it meant they could keep you with them forever. There is a reason why anytime you see a genie depicted he says that he can't make someone fall in love with you.

Wiccan love spells help you find your true love and to find love within yourself, for yourself. These loves spells are within basic moral rights and are encouraged. There is a thin line between morality, and immorality and love spells walk that line frequently.

Moonlight Love Attraction Spell

This spell is designed to help you attract love in your direction. While it may not bring you your true love right away, it will bring you people worth loving. You want to use this spell to help you bring in love to your life. Trying to restrict the spell can make it fail in strange ways.

What you need

pink candle

love attraction oil

matches

a full moon

Cast your circle, stand in the middle. Anoint the candle with the love attraction oil, and light it with the matches. Make sure that your circle is in the light of the moon, and say this chant

Goddess of grace

fertility and love

look down on me from up above

grace me with

resounding happiness

and give me love

nothing less

this is what I beg of you

take my life and make me anew

176

After you have said this spell, let the candle burn itself out in the light of the moon, while you sit meditating. Mentally send out your petition for love while you meditate. Once the candle has burnt out, close your circle, and gather up your items, and properly dispose of the stuff that you used up.

Finding Your Ideal Partner

This spell will help you find your true love. You want to use this spell with caution, and do not think of anyone in particular while you use it. You must come into a spell blank slate. Otherwise, you could end up with a faulty love spell.

What you need

- pink candle
- yellow candle
- white candle
- matches

To begin, first set up your pink, yellow, and white candles in a triangle. Once you do that, cast your circle. Light each candle using a new match each time. Once you have lit them, say this spell

I ask you o great ones

hear my cry

find me the one

who is to complete my life

I leave my trust

In you alone

bring my one true love into my home.

Once you have done this, you can blow out the candles, and watch the smoke dissipate. Once all the smoke is gone, you can close your circle, and clean up.

Spice Up Your Relationship

If you are in a relationship and you are anything like most couples, after the first year, things seem to get a little boring, and though you may love your significant other, you want some more excitement in your life. You are not alone in feeling this way. Everyone wants to spice things up a bit, but a lot of times, they do not know how or are too scared to do so. This spell will help bring things back to life in the bedroom. This magic involves the use of both herbs and candles, so make sure that you break out your herbs as well.

What you need

- cinnamon

- hibiscus

- carnation

- pink candle

- red candle

- matches

- mortar and pestle

- fireproof bowl

To begin this spell, crush your herbs together with your mortar and pestle, and pour them into a fireproof bowl. Once you have those ready, cast your circle. Light your red and pink candles with the same match. Say this spell after you have lit your candles

Love so tired

love is old

take my love and make it bold

As you say *bold* take your red candle and light the herbs. Let about half of them burn, before blowing it out. Then finish the spell with this

Bring back butterflies

banish the tears

give me fun

for the rest of our years

As you say *years*, take the pink candle and light the remaining herbs. Let the herbs burn out completely, and then blow out your candles before closing your circle.

Money Spells

Money spells are not what you are thinking. You will not become a millionaire if you are using magic, and if you are planning on trying to, you should put this book down now before getting disappointed. If you know someone who claims magic made them rich, then they used black magic, and are paying the price for it.

Use these spells with practical intentions, not out of this world dreams because they will never meet your expectations. The spells in this book are designed to only work for someone who wishes to use them as they are meant to be used. That is, to help you gain success and make more money.

Quick Pocket Change Spell

This spell is to help you find more extra money in your life, such as pennies, nickels, dimes, and even quarters. This spell will not gain you hundred dollar bills, and if you find one, then you should probably look for someone who might have dropped it. Riches is not what this spell is for.

What you need

- ⚔ green candle

- ⚔ money attracting oil

- ⚔ a coin

To do this spell, cast your circle. Anoint your candle with the money attraction oil towards you. Light your candle, and let a few drips drop onto the coin, being careful not to burn yourself (quarters seem to be the best for this as they have a bigger surface area). Use the wax on the coin to secure the candle to the coin. As it burns down, say this spell

Green candle,

bringer of money

I don't need much

just what you can spare me

a quarter here

a dime there

even some pennies

if you have some to spare

I beg of you

what you can give

I thank you now

in advance

Once the candle has burnt out, then you can close your circle, and remove the remnants of the candle from your coin. Keep as much melted wax on it as you can and then put the coin where you normally keep your change. Watch the change roll in.

Banishing Money Blocks

This spell helps you banish any obstacles in your way, such as debt. You may find after using this spell that some of your debt has been forgiven, or that something happened and a collection company lost your file, so you no longer owe. If you do not have a job, you may find that the job you have been waiting for is hiring. There are many ways this spell can work, so if it doesn't work in the way you want it too, don't be discouraged, because it may just be working on something else that is even better for you.

What you need

- green candle

- 3 pieces of paper

- fireproof bowl

To start this spell, cast your circle. Invite the elements to join you in this spell, don't just ask them to protect you while you do the spell. Fold the three pieces of paper into three separate cubes, and place them into the fireproof bowl. These cubes represent the money "blocks" in your way. Light the green candle, and say this spell

Fire of might

I ask of thee

to get these evil blockages

away from me

After you have said the spell, then take the green candle, and light the blocks on fire. Once they have burned out, blow out your green candle, and close your circle, thanking the element for joining you.

Healing Spells

Healing spells are a little more difficult, so the ones that are mentioned in this book, are going to be for the basic relief of ailments such as sprains, colds, or depression. These ailments are easily relieved with simple spells that do not require expert skills. Healing spells often require the green candle as well.

Simple Healing Spell

This spell is for your personal use. Use it to heal yourself from a sprain, or just the common cold. This spell is fairly effective, and you will find yourself experiencing relief in no time.

What you need

- green candle

- chamomile

- nutmeg

- lavender

- matches

- tea bag

- hot water

- cup

You do not need to cast a circle for this spell unless your injury is kind of deep. For basic ailments, you can just do these steps without a circle.

Light the green candle and say this spell

Candle of green

make me well

Tea of many leaves

make me well

so, I say

so, mote it be

Once you have lit the candle and said the spell, you can make your tea with the herbs mentioned above and drink it.

Banishing Depression Spell

This spell helps banish depression. While it does not cure depression, and if you struggle with it, you should seek professional help, it does help with the day to day struggles, such as just getting out of bed in the morning.

What you need

- yellow candle

- yellow ribbon long enough for a bracelet

Cast your circle and light the yellow candle. This spell does not need you to speak for anything other than to cast your circle. Take the ribbon and make it into the size of a bracelet that will slide on and off your wrist with ease, but will not fall off at any time without effort. Once you have found the perfect size, then burn the ends of the bracelet together to make a seam. Blow out the candle, and hold the bracelet in the smoke, until the smoke dissipates. Slide the bracelet back on and positive thoughts.

Section 4

Enhancing Your Life with Spells

The purpose of learning to be a witch is to enhance your life. You can do this with magic. You can find yourself entirely engulfed in a new and more adventurous lifestyle. Enhancing your life with magic takes a lot of practice.

Magic is not something that comes easily to most people. It takes getting out of your head to achieve anything. Life enhancement is a big part of the Wiccan culture, and that is what draws a lot of people to it. However, despite a lot of people being drawn to this religion, there are a lot of people that leave it as well, and that is because they are not willing to put in the effort when it comes to enhancing their lives. They expect just to say a few phrases and the magic happens. This is due in part to how the media portrays magic. Look at the popular television series *Charmed*. It shows three witches who fight evil, and all they do is use a few simple spells, and that is not reality. The same goes for most literature out there. Wiccans are portrayed as people who get together in the woods, say a few spells, wave a few herb sticks, and boom—magic. It is harder than these portrayals.

Spells take practice and require executing multiple times to master results. There are also several different parts to spells that you must master, once mastered; you get to move on to the next level and practice those spells for hours on end before you get any results. To become a powerful witch, you must put in a lot of time and be dedicated to your craft. The cost of being lazy will have you remain at the same level for ages.

You cannot expect life enhancement to make your life one of leisure. This is yet another reason people leave Wicca. They expect to be able to make their crush fall in love with them and to use magic to become rich, and that just doesn't happen—at least not right away. Those things take hard work and dedication.

People have also joined and fell off the wagon, by becoming black witches. They found out ways to make themselves rich, and force someone to fall in love with them. However, that magic comes at a price, and the price is not cheap. These people will literally sell their souls to a demon to achieve what they want. You want to stay away from these witches. If one were to die from a black witch, their soul would be tortured for all eternity. You will not be reincarnated; you will be sent straight to purgatory. Purgatory is where the spirits of people who have done evil things and used black magic go to in the afterlife. It is not where you want to end up. Your spirit will be torn to pieces every day until the end of time, and even though your body will be dead, you will still be alive to feel it because you are your spirit. Let those who join Wicca and turn to black witches' parish on their own accord.

Anyways, how do you enhance your life with magic? You connect with the earth. You connect with other people. You fill your life with things that will enrich you and bring you joy. These things are possible with magic. It may seem that magic can't do anything that you can't do yourself, and maybe there may be some truth to that. However, being in the Wiccan religion, it makes it a lot easier to do these things with magic, rather than without magic.

Here's how magic can help you enhance your life:

Making Friends - Friends are hard to come by, and even if you have a big group of friends, they may not be the best of friends to have. As humans, we are attracted to what are known as shiny people. These are usually the people that are fun to hang out with. However, these shiny people are generally not the best people to be around, as they seem only to hang around if you can do something for them. Humans are also easily drawn in by dramatic people. These people are the ones that are always loud, and always doing something that they shouldn't be doing. It is exciting, and it is fun. However, if they turn on you, it can be an unpleasant experience. These people can be toxic, and toxicity is the best way to ruin a friendship. You want to hang onto these people because you think that they bring a lot of joy to your life, but the truth is they are only dragging you down. Usually, people feel obligated at the requests of shiny people—starting to ring any bells? To spot a toxic friend all you should do is try to do something that you want to do for yourself or ask for a favor, and watch them try to drag you down or not participate.

This is where magic comes in. Magic will draw in the right type of friends so that you can make a lasting bond with them, and not have to worry about them walking out of your life because you reach a milestone in your life, and can't take them to the mall twenty times a week anymore. Instead, these friends will root for you, encourage you to be the best that you can be, and they will not bat an eye when you do something to improve your life.

Magic will help you find the love of your life and someone who will bring you soup when you are sick. You will attract the type of person who doesn't care if you are wearing your pajamas all day or wearing a $300 dress when you see them. These friends are hard to come by, and magic will fill your life with these friends. This way you can ensure that you are making friends with the right kind of people.

Help You Find True Love - True love is the hardest to find. You may fall in love several times in your life, and you may even get married, but chances are it is not everlasting love. Love is everywhere, and at times can be easy to find. However, the true love hard to find, because they are not looking for the right identifiers. They want excitement and butterflies forever, and while those are all well and good to have with your partner twenty years from now, the butterflies eventually fade, or they will not happen as frequently. When that happens, you want to still be able to wake up and kiss the person beside you good morning and feel good about it. If you don't, how will you ever love them for the rest of your life? Find someone who even when the butterflies fade, gives you a warm feeling in your heart, and makes you happy. True love is the love where you can argue all day, and then laugh and be happy for months on end. True love is waking up next to the one you love, and seeing them in their most vulnerable state, and loving them even more. This love is the love that people strive for endlessly, and it is a love that not a lot of people find. Some are tricked into thinking they found it because the butterflies last longer than usual, then they get married, and five years later, they get a divorce. This is because they just found someone that they lusted after longer than usual.

Enter magic. Magic will bring you someone who can make your heart race, and make you feel calm at the same time. It will bring you the person who will hold your hair when you are sick, and rub your feet when they are sore. It will bring you, someone, who will help with the dishes for the rest of your life. Someone who gets up with you at two in the morning to bake cookies when you can't sleep.

You want someone who is encouraging of the Wiccan religion so that you can be yourself around them. Once you let go and let fate show you who you should truly be with, these spells will help take your relationships, and make them strong, and at the same time help you form a bond with someone to create an unbreakable relationship. Letting fate take over is the hardest part. You want to find someone who you like, but most people do not trust fate to make that choice because they already have someone in mind to be their forever love. They do not want to relinquish that control for fear of something going away. Are you going to fall in love with someone who is truly the one for you, or are you going to spend the rest of your life fighting with the person you married, and using countless spells to try to fix your relationship? The choice is for you alone, but with a little patience, and a little time, you will find the person that you have truly been waiting for.

Courage - If you are a person who is not particularly courageous in any aspect of life, do not fret. You are not alone. The average person has at least one area in their life where they lack in the courage department. This can range from being talking to strangers, or trying to make it up in the business ladder. There are many parts of life that require courage; it is impossible to be courageous enough for all of them on your own. For instance, you may be able to go skydiving, but the thought of talking to that gorgeous person who has caught your eye completely terrifies you. And that is okay because you can't be courageous at everything. Or maybe you are great at talking to people, and doing public speaking, but you are terrified to ride an elevator. There are different fears out there, and you cannot conquer your fears without courage. A lot of people overlook magic and how it can boost your courage levels up. Courage is important, and spells can make you a little stronger. As a witch, it is one of the most important things you can have because you are going to have to stand up to people. Whether it be to save an old tree from a company that wants to tear it down, or stopping a black witch from ruining someone's life, lots of acts require courage.

Magic can help, and it can bring you so much more than a little bit of courage. Magic can make you feel like you can take on the world. You will feel like you can do anything, and that is what you want. Just remember that the effects are not permanent, and you may have to reapply the spell a couple of times. Magic gives you the courage until you find it on your own, after a few times of realizing how great it feels to stand up to something that terrifies you, you will not need the spell anymore because you will be able to be courageous on you own.

Luck - Luck is hard to come by, and lots of people need it. You need luck when you are playing the lottery, and you need luck when you ask the love of your life to marry you, and that is something that not a lot of people think of either. Just like courage, luck is something that you need to get by in life. It is not always hard work that you should rely on because sometimes, hard work can only get you so far. Such as in a big law firm, where you and the partner's pet are vying for a promotion. You may do the harder jobs, and work the hardest, but they have the advantage on you because they are a favorite. In this case, a little luck may help. Luck can ensure that they are paying attention to your hard work, rather than having a clear winner picked out before the race even begins.

You can use a few simple spells to make talismans and good luck charms, as well as just cover yourself in an aura of good luck with some spells; these spells are generally not difficult. However, the more luck you desire, the stronger the witch you would have to be, because, the stronger the witch, the more powerful the spell. You also have to "reapply" less when you are more powerful. Even more, reason to practice, right? Everyone wants to be lucky, so make sure to work on becoming the best witch that you can be.

A real-life scenario would be a job interview. You want to use these spells without abandon, because the more luck you have, the better off you will be in an interview, and you will hopefully land the job with ease. Don't get too cocky, even though you may apply and interview, if you are not a good fit, you may not get the job no matter how much magic you use.

Recall there is a major difference between confidence and being cocky. Confidence is knowing you can do the job. Being cocky is thinking that without any training you can do it better than everyone else. Cocky is thinking that you are a shoe-in for a job you have never had any experience with. Confidence is knowing that you are a strong and quick learner and will be good at the job without any training. You want to be confident, yet humble. Know that you are not the perfect person for the job, but also know that you are the best candidate.

Clarity of Mind - Have you ever had a question that is burning in your mind or a decision that you had to make that was really hard? Did it take you longer than you care to admit to achieve what you wanted with these scenarios? That happens to everyone at some point in their life, and it is entirely normal. You want to have a clear mind, and it is harder to achieve than you would think. And, even if you clear your mind, a lot of times it is still hard to find a clear answer. You search and search, but there are pros and cons to everything. This makes it hard to find yourself the time to do what you want to do when you want to do it because you are still agonizing over making the decision or trying to figure everything out—decisions can be messy.

If you are having trouble figuring out where to go in life, you can use a spell to help you figure things out. There are many spells that help you open your mind to make the right decision, and a lot of it has to do with Divination. Yes, prophesying helps you make the right choices because you will be able to get an idea of what will be the outcome of your choice. There are spells out there to clear your mind, and there are spells to get the answers that you desire. These spells are the ones that you want to use to find your way in life and really make the right choices. Perhaps you are wondering if your spouse is cheating, and you do not know if you should pursue the matter. Do a spell and get the answers you are looking for. Don't feel guilty if they are not cheating. You are not going through their personal effects, rather doing your research before confronting them and that is what a rational person does.

Banishing Evil - Let's face it, a lot of times, we are surrounded by evil. This world is a demonic playground, no doubt about it. In these times, it becomes harder to find a pure environment, and a lot of times those who are good are under attack from the world. Have you ever felt like the entire world was against you, and even though the evil people seem to be living good lives, you are miserable? That is what a lot of people deal with when they try to lead decent lives because it seems that life does not want good in it and rewards evil. There are ways to keep yourself pure and keep your environment pure as well. Have a good place to do your magic. You want your mind to be pure and clean from attacks of other, evil witches as well.

There are several spells out there for purifying not only the area but your mind as well. One of the most common spell types for purification is known as smudging.

Smudging is covered in *Wicca: Herbal Magic*. It is the process of burning a stick of herbs to purify an area or achieve the effects of any other plethora of spells. Burning herbs have a powerful effect and create a magical barrier around you. This barrier is great for the place that you choose to do your magic, so make sure you purify that area regularly because the barrier does not last forever— unfortunately.

If you are practicing regularly, you should probably smudge your area before each spell, but if you are not practicing often, once a week or biweekly should suffice. Just make sure that you purify it before you do a spell. The purer you keep it, the more effect your spells will have on your life and evil forces will not be able to counteract your spells. There are several other spells that you can use to make sure that you are keeping your mind and environment pure from the evil that lurks around. Candles are essential to this (white candles especially). They give you a pure energy in which to perform your spells with. White candles act as a channel directly to the Goddess herself to help you keep other entities from answering your calls. Although most spells do not call for white candles, it is best to light one whenever you do a spell.

Healing - As you a Wicca beginner, you can relieve side effects and many other issues that dwell under and on top of the surface of one's skin. Mental illnesses are something that you can help with. While you cannot cure these diseases, you can help alleviate the symptoms of things such as depression and anxiety. You can also help someone who has PTSD sleep better at night. Magic when used to help people, including yourself, is wonderful. It also does not take a lot of magical strength to help alleviate the symptoms of illnesses, unlike with pain and suffering from a major physical injury.

Prosperity - Have you ever been unemployed and found yourself searching high and low for any source of income just to keep the lights on? It isn't fun, and nowadays it is getting harder to find jobs that are enough to pay the bills and keep food on the table. That is the downside of the world we live in. Jobs are becoming electronic and outsourced. And unfortunately, unless you live in a commune, you must have money to survive.

There are a lot of spells to help you have the upper hand with prosperity. It is a good idea to find a plethora of them to douse yourself with luck and prosperity if you are ever in need of it. The same goes with healing spells.

Magic is a great life enhancer. It will give you the boost you need to accomplish great things in different arenas of life. Use Wicca magic to aid you on your journey here. You do not want to use it to make your life. Put in the effort and the magic will give you a leg up that you may not have had on your own. That is the beautiful thing about Wicca magic. It is not there to be a crutch, but rather a tool to help you succeed.

Wicca

Altar

Wiccan Tools for Spells and Casting Your Circle

Valerie W. Holt

A Brief Introduction

This book is part of a five-book series on Wiccan culture. It is very important that you read the other books along with this one to immerse yourself in the religion and learn more about it. In this book, you will find slightly different information than what appears in the others, as this book is about the tools you will need as a Wiccan.

Section 1

The Wiccan Altar

Origin of the Altar

The altar is a very important part of the Wiccan culture. It is a raised object on which a Wiccan places ritual tools and offerings to the gods and goddesses above. It is the place of worship to the deities that control the lives of Wiccans, and it is a very sacred place. However, the altar has been many things over time; some people use a table, some people build a pyre, but it all depends on how old-fashioned you want to go and how much you want to put on your altar.

The altar dates back to ancient times and is highly revered, though in today's age many people are drifting away from the traditional altar to perform their spells faster. In days past, the altar was used for every single spell; you would put all your tools for the spell on the altar, along with any offerings needed. These offerings were generally burnt food, or coins or herbs. In true Wiccan culture, sacrifices are banned. The only bloodletting is from the person performing the spell.

The Wiccan altar is a mix of the Pagan altar and the Christian altar. The Pagan altar was used for sacrifices as well as offerings and was often tainted with blood. Even if the Pagan were not worshiping Satan, he/she would still kill animals for spells. The Christian altar is for the pastor to place his Bible on, along with anything else needed for the sermon. The altar was prayed upon by the people of the church and was often important when tithe buckets were passed around. The altar was not used for any other offering but money.

In the old Catholic Testament, the first altar was used to make an animal sacrifice. When Jesus died for the sins of man, sacrifices were deemed unclean. With that in mind, the Christian altar is not as clean as it may seem today. However, the cleanliness that we see in Christian altars today influenced Wiccan altars as we know them.

The Pagan Altar idea of keeping all one's tools used for the spell on the altar so as to keep them sacred is also integrated into the Wiccan altar. This is so your tools do not touch the ground or anything that may affect their purity, as you must say a consecration prayer over your altar. Because the altar is consecrated, it will help keep your tools consecrated as well.

The Wiccan altar is very important in traditional rituals, so if a spell calls for an altar, you should use one (even if it is just a table or mound of earth with a cloth) so that you can say a consecration prayer over it. There are so many ways you can use an altar; often you do not have to build one yourself if you have ANYTHING that can keep your tools off the unconsecrated ground.

Creating Your Altar

There are many ways you can create your own altar. You just have to find something that is raised off the ground. Here is a list of things you can use for your altar, and how good they are to use.

Cardboard Box: This is something a lot of people use; they just cover it with a cloth and say a consecration prayer. In a pinch, this is a good idea, but it has its cons, and most of them have to do with natural energy. Cardboard is a processed product, meaning bare natural material did not go into making it. If you can find recycled cardboard, that is a little better, but it is still processed, which can create issues that interfere with natural magical energy. You do not want any problems with your spells, so if you have any other option, it is best that you do not use a box.

Wooden Pallet: These are used a lot by Wiccans who love to reuse things, and it is actually a good idea. Pallets are made from raw wood and are not super processed, making them purer; thus, they will not mess with the energy of the magic. You want to have a pure altar if you can, and this is as close to being pure as you can get. Just make sure to sand it down because pallets are rough and can snag your cloth, causing rips or tears. You do not want a tear in your cloth because it will cause a tear in the spell.

Table: Some people use tables, ranging from plastic card tables to hand-crafted wood tables. A table can be a great altar if it is made from real wood. Just as with the cardboard, processed plastic is good in a pinch, but if you have anything made from a material closer to the raw substance, it is best to use that. Because plastic is not a raw material, it can affect the energy of your spell, and that is not a good thing because you want your spell to be as strong as possible. A raw wood table is a great altar, much like a stack of pallets would be. You want the wood to be as raw and untreated as possible but, again, make sure the wood is smooth, so you do not tear your cloth.

Mound of Earth: If you can find a nice mound of earth, it is a great idea to use this for an altar. However, you must consecrate it every time you use it because it is out in nature and can be disturbed by other energies in the world. On the bright side, a consecration prayer is easy to do and does not take that long. It is even faster if you have holy water. You want to be as pure as possible, and this is as raw as it gets. When it comes to altars, you couldn't get more close to nature than if you were a tree yourself. Make sure the mound is big and smooth enough on top to hold your tools properly. You do not want them rolling onto the unconsecrated ground.

Boulder: If you cannot find a mound of earth but can find a nice boulder, this will also work well as a raw altar. Again, make sure you consecrate it every time or else other energies of the world could taint it, especially if an evil person used it as a place of rest. There are so many ways that the energies of natural products can be tainted, so it is always better to be safe than sorry because you do not want the energy of your spell to be tainted. Tainted spell energy can lead to a faulty or disastrous spell, and that is not a good thing to have happen.

Tree Stump: As with a mound of earth or a boulder, a tree stump makes a great altar once consecrated, as it is raw and natural and will hold energy more than a processed product will. The tree itself was once alive, so it has energy it can add to your spell to make it stronger. A tree stump is probably even better than a mound of earth because of how much energy a tree possesses even after it is cut; even though the top is cut, the tree may still be alive if the roots are not dead. This energy will strengthen your spell up to 100 times, so be careful if you do not want your spell to be too strong.

These are some of the things you can use as an altar. The altar is an important part of Wiccan rituals, so it is always a good idea to have one on hand in case you need to perform an old-fashioned ritual.

Consecration Spell for Your Altar

If you want to have an altar but need a consecration spell for one and don't know where to turn, here is a basic one. It involves holy water, so make sure you have some on hand. You can often buy holy water online. Remember that when you are doing a consecration spell, you must have only pure thoughts in your head. It is easiest to think of the color white when you are doing this spell, so if you have trouble figuring out what thoughts are pure vs. impure, just imagine a white sheet. It helps a lot.

What you need

- holy water
- tablecloth the color of the spell type

Place the tablecloth on your altar, and sprinkle it with holy water. As you are flicking the holy water onto the altar, say this prayer:

Mother Goddess let me be seen

Make my altar pure and clean

Say this until the entire altar has been anointed with holy water. Once you have finished, you are ready to move on to using your altar.

Using Your Altar

When you use your altar, you must make sure you have all the tools on hand because you must set them on the altar at the beginning of the spell. You cannot set them there once the spell has begun because they will disrupt the magical energies. Make sure you are organized and have everything you need to get the job done; otherwise you will have some issues with spell energy, and no one wants that.

Place your tools on the altar clockwise in the order you will use them. If you need a chalice, it always goes in the center, while an athame always goes at the six o'clock position. Offerings go at the twelve o'clock position. If you do not have any of those things, go on with the order in which they will be used, the first being at the twelve o'clock position and the last being at the nine o'clock position (or eleven if you have more than four items).

When you perform a spell, always walk up to the front of your altar, never try to grab your items from the back. The front of the altar is the six o'clock position. You must make sure you are standing in the center front of the altar and not to one side. That will leave your spell unbalanced. You must always be mindful of where you are located when it comes to a positioning in your spell so that you do not knock into your altar or approach it from the wrong side.

When you are done with the spell, you must remove the tools counterclockwise starting with the last thing used and working your way around the altar. If you have a chalice, remove it last. Offerings are to be left in the area in which you did your spell, so they will be taken off the altar just before you take it away unless your altar is nature. For everything else, remove it counterclockwise.

Aligning Energies

The outside world can interfere with your energies in your spells if you do not protect yourself from them. The clashing energies can even nullify a spell or make it go haywire and become disastrous. You must do your best to avoid this catastrophe and make sure you are moving your energies in sync with the world around you. The only problem is, when you are doing a spell, you cannot also align the energies because your focus is on the spell.

How do you keep the outside world from interfering? You cast a circle, of course. This is one of the easiest ways to align your energy with the world and block out negativity and interference. Casting a circle is relatively easy, and there are several ways you can do it. You can mark out your circle, pentagram and all. You can mark it out with candles, or you can choose not to mark it out at all. This is entirely up to you. All that matters is that you cast a circle to protect yourself and your spell.

You must align your energies to have a safe space as well. If you do not have a circle cast, you will have problems with entities other than the deities finding their way into your rituals. Most spells you do will need to have a circle cast. The exception is with charms. They are not strong enough to get the attention of any demonic entities, so you will be safe not casting a circle with them.

If you align your energies well, you will be able to perform a spell and make it stronger than you could if you were using just your own energy. The energy alignment will help boost your spell into the cosmos and make it rebound faster and stronger than it would have otherwise. Be careful with love spells, as if the spell is too strong it could go horribly awry.

The Altar and The Circle

The altar should be at the center of the circle. Many people try to put it outside the circle, but if you do that the circle does not protect it. The altar is the pinnacle of a spell, and it is where the spirit resides, so it should be in the center, where you would go to call a spirit to your circle.

When you set up your altar, make sure it is consecrated. If it is not, you could have some issues with making the spell work. All altars must be consecrated to work well.

Section 2

The Tools of Wiccan Rituals and Magic

There are many tools out there that witches use in the Wiccan religion. These tools help with everything from basic spells to intricate rituals. These tools are very important in the culture and should be treated as such. Many new-age witches look with disdain upon some of the tools when they must use them and then wonder why their spells did not work as well as they had hoped. You must respect the magical items you use for your rituals. They hold energy, and that energy reacts well only to positive energy. If you come into a ritual with negative energy towards a magical tool, the tool will react negatively because it does not have the proper reaction with the witch's energy.

You want a good reaction with your tools to make sure all your spells go as planned. If you do not have a good reaction, your spell may not work or will work poorly. With that in mind, always respect your altar and everything that lays upon it.

The Basics
Altar Cloths

The altar cloth is one of the most important things on your altar. It is your barrier between negative energies and your consecrated tools. It is what you use to set the entire tone of the spell, so you should use a cloth color that coordinates with your spell. If you cannot decide what color you need, you can always choose white because it is neutral. However, certain colors work best with some spells. Here is a quick rundown of them.

Blue: This color is for spells that increase wisdom. There are several spells for which you will need an altar, and that will benefit from having a blue altar cloth. Blue is also helpful with stressful situations in which you often find yourself. The blue of the cloth will help your spell and boost the energy to make it more ironclad. You want to use this cloth when you are trying to retain information when studying for a big test or when you want to learn more about a certain subject. This is a great color for any knowledge you want to obtain.

Green: This is great for prosperity spells. Green is a good money attractor due to it being the color of money. It is full of the energy of prosperity and success. These spells can help you land a job or bring you more pocket change. If you want to ensure that you have a prosperous life and that your spells work as well as they possibly can, you should make sure that you are using a green altar cloth. This cloth is best for spells you would use to create more success at your job. However, prosperity is not the only thing this color will help with. It will help with healing as well.

Pink: This is the color of love. Cloth in this color would be for a powerful love spell. Love spells are very volatile, so having an altar cloth that is pink is very important, as it will add grounding and a stabilizing energy to your spell. If you do not use a pink cloth, use a white one for its neutral energy (though it will not be able to stabilize as well as a pink one). Pink is almost exclusively for love spells and success in your love life. If you feel that you are not where you want to be in your love life, you could try a spell to boost your life in a good way. Such a spell can attract the people you want to be around and ensure that you find the person you need, not necessarily the person you want.

White: This is the color of purity. A white altar cloth is for when you are not sure what color you need for your spell, or when you just want a purifying energy added to your spell. White altar cloths represent balance, safety, and cleanliness.

There are many other colors you can use for altar cloths, such as red, purple, orange, and yellow. These colors have different magical meanings. The power of color is more substantial than you might think; it can affect what you are doing with your spell.

Altar Candles

Altar candles are candles you place on your altar, and they provide light as part of your ritual. They are often white unless you need colors to represent the elements. These candles are lit as you are performing the ritual unless the ritual calls for them to be lit as you cast your circle. These candles are not to be confused with candles you use to mark out your circle, as they are entirely different and are not to leave the altar for any reason.

When you place the altar candles, pay attention to the number of candles you have. This will determine the placement of the candles, as they should be positioned in a certain way for a certain number. If you have only one candle, it should go in the twelve o'clock position, in front of the magical object you have placed there, closest to the edge of the altar. If you have two candles, use twelve and six o'clock – the same placement. If you have four candles, place one on each corner of the altar (twelve, three, six, nine if your altar is round). If you have five candles, you should have one on each corner and one in the middle. Notice that there are no instructions for three candles. You should never have three candles. Magic is all about balance and three is an unbalanced number.

Deity Representation

Some Wiccans like to represent the deities on their altars. This is entirely optional, and as of late has become a practice that is not really defined in the way of rituals. Often, the representations are little statues that you would place on your altar. They typically go in the middle of the sides if you are using a square altar or at ten and two if you are using a round altar.

If you use a deity representation, make sure the statue has been consecrated so that only the deity the statue represents will answer the call of your spell. Otherwise, the statue will draw in other entities as well because they see you as a more vulnerable target, believing that if you have the representation, you believe that only those deities can answer the call. This is not the case. If statues are consecrated, then yes, that is true. If they are unconsecrated, they create a break in your circle, inviting in the wrong entities.

Athame

This is a decorative sacrificial knife that you will find in many rituals in Wiccan traditions. These are not used in a lot of spells for which you actually have to cut yourself; however, for a few older-style spells, you do. In many new-age spells, you use the knife to "cut" a symbol into the air and really seal a spell.

Athames are often silver, for the deity Gaea, and have a moon and a pentagram etched on the hilt. They are curved and generally six inches long. They are not very big, but they should be kept sharp and shiny. If they are needed, they go in the middle of your altar along with the chalice you will probably need.

Wand

In many movies about witches and wizards, the wand is portrayed as the source of power. You must have a wand to do anything. In these movies, you can see a ball of energy fly out of the end of the wand, and you see grandiose displays of magic. Wands are generally the pivotal point of the magic, and without them, the wizard or witch is essentially useless. Take *Harry Potter and the Chamber of Secrets*, in which Ron Weasley's wand gets broken as he tries to get the car to move out of the Whomping Willow. Throughout the rest of the movie, his spells backfire or go disastrously wrong. When he tries to perform an "eat slugs" spell on his rival, Ron ends up being the one eating slugs, and when his teacher tries to use Ron's wand to wipe his memory, the spell hits the teacher instead.

However, in the real culture of Wicca, wands are not the pivotal point from which magic is released. In fact, for most spells, wands are merely decorative. If you do need a wand, it is merely to concentrate your magic into one area. This is the most significant thing for which you will use a wand. However, wands are still important in the culture, and you will make your own. First, you must find wood that speaks to you. It is best to cut your wand directly from a tree to have the strongest magic, but if you do not have any good trees around you, carving a wand from an already-cut piece of wood works too.

Once you have found good wood for your wand, you must wake up the magic within using an awakening spell. This will bring your wand into the magical realm and awaken the energies that pulsate within the wood. You can hollow it out and add a core if you like, but this is not necessary.

Chalice

A chalice is a decorative cup that you use in a ceremony during which you must drink something or pour a liquid onto the ground as an offering to the deities. This is not just a boring foam cup, however; it is something you should take care in choosing. Many Wiccan supply stores have different chalice styles, and you can choose the one that suits you.

Chalices look like decorative metal wine glasses with symbols carved into them, and possibly gemstones around the rim and the base. They do not have to be super expensive; you just have to make sure you are not being lazy and getting any old cup. Chalices are generally used only in sacred rituals, so it is best to keep them as nice as possible.

They must be hand washed and consecrated after every use. Do not defile one by putting it in the dishwasher or forgetting to consecrate it after washing it with regular water. Though they may not be used often, chalices are important because they are the basis of many age-old rituals. To disrespect the chalice is to disrespect the deities themselves.

You should have a chalice with markings similar to your athame. A matched set is best, as it represents balance in your altar, and magic is all about balance in the world. If it is on your altar, your spell will have more power, as it does not have to fight an imbalance.

Element Representation

Often, Wiccans represent the elements on their altars, either with actual representation or color representation with stones, candles, etc. The best way to represent the elements is through actual representation, meaning the use of actual objects to represent an element.

The best way to represent air is through incense, as the smoke is taken by the air to fill the area with a good smell. To represent air, simply light the incense as you call air to your circle, then watch the smoke dance in the wind.

Air is the element of power yet subtlety, and it is the first element you would call to your circle. You must call air with certainty, as a wavering voice might cause air not to respond. Be strong and firm, and allow your representation to show that you respect the element enough to entice it into your circle.

Incense of any kind is a great way to call air; scents that are light and fresh are the best. Look for "breeze" in the title and make sure the incense is 100% natural; otherwise, air might get offended by the fact that you are calling it with chemically created incense.

If you want to call fire to your circle using a representation, a candle is a great way to go. The flame of the candle is strong yet gentle enough to show that you are willing to allow fire to work without interference. Fire is a finicky element and does not like to be messed with. If you are representing fire, a cinnamon candle is the best way to go.

The element of fire represents passion; fire is the element of spontaneity, as you never know how fast or slow a fire will move if it will stay tame or blow up and cause mass destruction. Fire is a beautiful yet dangerous element, and that seems to be what makes it so enticing. You must call fire to your circle with caution; be careful not to offend, as fire will make your spell strong or destroy it all depending on how much respect you show the element.

As volatile and unstable as fire is, if you call it in second and call the other elements shortly afterward, you will have a balance that will keep fire in check. The time between when you call fire and then call the final element, spirit, is crucial because that is when fire is going to react if it is offended.

To represent water, all you need is a dish of water. Tap water will suffice, but water straight from a river or ocean is better. Stay away from bottled water, as the elements do not take kindly to people using processed items to call them. The purest form you can get is the best way to go; however, you must make sure it is fresh. You cannot gather sea water into a jug and use it two months later because that is as bad as a processed bottled water representation. The water must constantly be moving, and you are hurting it by keeping it trapped like an animal in a cage. Use it for a short time and then release it back to where it came from.

The element of water is gentle, yet it can be powerful if it needs to be. The same water that can cleanse your skin can cause a violent and unpleasant death moments later. The water that sustains our bodies can, when angered, ravage and destroy homes in the blink of an eye. Yes, that is what causes floods; the element has been angered and lets its fury loose on the people who have angered it, sometimes harming civilians in the process. Of course, there is actual science behind this, but there is religion as well because the two can coexist, contrary to popular belief.

When representing water, make sure you respect the element as you would the others; just because it is gentle most of the time does not mean it is not dangerous, nor that it cannot be offended. You must realize that water, just like any other element, is a wild, raw power that can destroy just as fast as it can build and sustain. When calling water, it is best to do so right after you call fire so the two elements can keep each other balanced under the watch of air.

Representing earth is one of the easiest things to do. This also means it is the easiest to mess up because you can overestimate how easy it is. You can represent earth with a bowl of sea salt or soil. If you are using sea salt, it is best to get it straight from the sea and evaporate the water from the salt. If you cannot get fresh sea salt, it is best to get soil that is straight from the earth. Including some grass in it helps as well. However, earth is one of the most sensitive elements of the five. Due to all the pollution nowadays, it is even more sensitive than before. Make sure you use only raw, natural ingredients when you are calling this element. It is best to collect the earth in a porcelain bowl.

Representing spirit is hard to do; the most-recommended tool to use is a purple veil. This represents spirit well, as it signifies the break between the human and spirit worlds. Spirit is very hard to upset, as it is often overlooked, and is very grateful to be represented in your altar. It is best to stay away from polyester veils if possible simply because they are very flammable and if you are representing the elements, you probably have candles going everywhere as well.

It is extremely important to show respect to the elements in your representation and when you call them to your circle. Otherwise, they will not answer your call, and you could be left vulnerable when doing your magic. However, the elements are generally eager to please and serve, so as long as you are polite, you should have no problems calling them in.

Anointing Oils

Oils are another important part of magical spells. Again, not all spells will call for oil, but a lot of them will call for at least one, if not more. You want to make sure you have several oils on hand in case you need them. You can even make your own. Look up what particular herbs do to make sure you are creating an oil that is suitable for your spell. You do not want to use lavender in a love spell, or mugwort in a dream spell.

You can also order pre-made oils, but there is a slight problem with this. Oils work best when they are used by the person who made them because the intention matches up 100 percent. Otherwise, there will be some misalignment of intention and the oil will not be as strong. It works in a pinch, though, if you are out of the oil you need and don't have six days to make new oil.

Book of Shadows

The first tool you need is a spirited book, also known as a book of shadows. The purpose of this book is to keep all your magical thoughts, spells, and creative ideas in one place, so they are easy to find. A book of shadows often contains spells and notations from a witch on magical things. The best part about a book of shadows is that it is all yours. You do not have to take someone else's book, study it, and learn what that person wants you to learn. Unlike with the Bible, you make your own book. It is your story, not someone else's.

There are several things you'll need to make a book of shadows. The first thing you need is an actual journal. Try to find something with actual leather. The leather will absorb energy and keep it alive. You want something that keeps the energy alive and the power locked inside. A paper-bound notebook is not as effective, which can cause problems with your spell book.

It is a common belief among Wiccans that one who has power over another's spellbook has power over that witch.

This is not a proven theory, but it is not something you would ever want to try out. Voodoo dolls work; your spellbook could become like a super powerful voodoo doll, and nobody wants that. Having someone take control of your body without your consent is no fun; you never want to experience that.

You want a spell book made with good leather. This will help keep the spell book's protective enchantments alive and moving. You do not want them to wear off.

You also need all the tools to create a protective enchantment in your spell book. These are going to be mentioned in a later chapter, so they will not be discussed here, but you will want to perform a protective spell. These spells are not that difficult if you are doing so just for a base level spell. Of course, higher lever spells are more complicated, but your spell book should need only a basic protection spell.

Once you have put a spell on your book, you must find a pen that you will use only with your spell book. You do not want cross contamination, as superstitious as that may sound. The outside world carries energies, and these energies are often tainted with interferences on the magical world. These interferences could nullify your protection spell. You do not want that, so it is best to find a pen you use specifically with your journal. The best way to go is with a fountain pen with an inkwell, but any pen will do. The fountain pen is simply more natural and keeps the whole Wicca theme going.

Once you have found a pen and a journal, you must make a note of where you found them because you will want to buy more. You won't have just one pen and journal your entire life. This is something many newbies do not understand. You must make sure you are not overfilling your journals. Also, many people think that you simply add more pages as you go along; while you can do this, there are some issues with this concept. The first is that these pages are not consecrated and are not completely covered by the protection spell. They may be protected while the pages are in the journal, but they are not when they fall out. This will leave the spells on that page vulnerable to being used by another witch, and if another witch uses a spell that has something to do with your personal life (one that is not a generic spell but made specifically for you), they can affect your life because that spell is tied to you. Monetary spells are the most delicate to use. Several are generic, but once you start adding prayers for a specific part of your life, that is where they become tricky.

Why You Need a Book

You do not need a book per se, but if you do not keep one and you leave personal spells lying around unprotected, you can open your life to a world of trouble. If you are just a magic dabbler, you should be fine finding generic spells and writing them down so that you can use them. However, if you plan on really immersing yourself in this culture, you must create some personal spells.

That is where a book of shadows comes in. It protects your personal spells and protects your life from chaos. You want to make sure that you are not letting your personal life get into the hands of something or someone who will try to destroy it. The book gives you a sanctified place to keep your spells, your thoughts on magic, and observations you have made in the magic world.

You also need a book if you want to join a coven, and even most circles require that you have a book. The reason is quite simple: organization. Covens often have synchronized books for meetings and then personal shadow books for their home use, but both are extremely organized so that people can easily find what they need.

A book of shadows is almost like a rite of passage for a Wiccan. Even though you do not absolutely need one, it is a good idea to get one, even if it simply means that you feel more at home with magic and makes you feel like you are one with the magical world.

Additional Options

Of course, there are other tools that are generally optional; most of the time they don't have a huge effect on the magic woven in your spell. They are merely decorative and make you feel more at home with magic. However, some spells do call for them, and in these spells, they DO affect the magic, so you should have them on hand in case you need them. This way, you can ensure that you are prepared for the spell and that you do not miss your opening in case it is time sensitive.

Broom

The broom is a symbol of strength in the Wiccan religion. Contrary to media portrayal, it is not something you can fly on. The broom is merely a decorative item, but sometimes you need it to "sweep" negative energy – or other magical energies you do not want interfering with your magic – out of your spell.

A witch's broom is wooden and has straw at its head. You do not want to use a store-bought broom, as it will not have any magical energy due to it's being processed. You will want to make your own or if you must buy one, get one from a Wiccan supply store, as their brooms are handmade and will have the energy you need.

If you decide to make your own, be sure that you sand down the handle because splinters are not a fun thing to deal with and you do not want to have any distractions when you are performing a spell. Splinters can prove to be a very big distraction, one that can throw off the balance of your magic.

Witch's Bell

Also known as a devil driver, this is a little decorative bell that wards off evil spirits in the magical realm. They were a big thing at the beginning of the Wiccan religion, but now they are not used very much, as most Wiccans do not believe that the devil exists. This is a big problem because it can lead these Wiccans to get too cocky with their magic and not use protective measures. The devil is real. He is not a little red man with a pointy tail and a pitchfork, but he is real, and he will try to mess with the purity of your magic and bring you to the dark side. A witch's bell should be rung seven times before you start your spell. This should be done in a circle around your circle to provide an extra layer of protection. Make sure you are not too hurried when you do this. You must let each strike of the bell resonate until it dies out before you move to the next position and ring the bell again.

Pentacle Slab

The pentacle slab is exactly what its name describes. It is a slab of a material with a pentagram engraved on it. Wood and stone are the most common materials, and they are very useful. The pentacle slab is used for protection of your spell, to make sure your spell goes where it is supposed to go and does not get in the hands of the wrong entity once it leaves your circle. You do not need a pentacle slab, but if you are a beginner in the magical world or are dabbling in gray magic, it is best to use this.

Incense Accessories

Incense can be a big part of your spells. Sometimes you need it for air representation, and sometimes you need it as part of the spell. If you use incense, there are some things you may need for it. These are completely optional, and there are several options to choose from. However, you do not have to choose any of these items if you do not want to other than something to hold up the incense, so it does not burn anything. The incense itself is all you need for the spell, and it must be able to stand upright so that it doesn't burn things and so the smoke can go into the air to work its magic.

If you do want to deck out your incense a little more, here are a few things that will help you out.

Incense Oil

This is like an essential oil, but it is made specifically to be drawn up through the stick of the incense to make the smell and the smoke a lot stronger. You can use it on smokeless incense as well, but most spells call for smoking incense, as the smoke (not the scent) is what performs the magic most of the time. This oil works with smoking incense too, though. Use it if you need a little extra kick to your spell, to make it really stick to the object you need it to.

Incense Holder

There are several types of holders, and they are all useful. There are decorative holders, and there are holders that are not pretty, but that get the job done. There are holders that allow you to add oil or rocks. These holders keep your incense upright and can make it more pleasing to the eye as well as more enticing to the deities. Ultimately, you simply need something that will hold your incense up, but if you can find a holder that does the trick and that looks nice, especially if it matches your chalice and athame, you should definitely go with it.

Ash Catcher

If you have ever burnt incense, you know how frustrating it is to clean up the ash it leaves behind. The ash from an incense stick is very fine and disintegrates when it is touched. This leaves you feeling more like you are spreading it around than cleaning it up. However, there are ash catchers that will help with that. You can even get an incense holder that has an ash catcher built in; that is super helpful because you will have fewer problems when it comes time to clean up after a spell.

These are just a few of the items you can get as accessories to incense, but these are the most essential. There are several other accessories that hold no other function than to be decorative. These items are not useful in your spell.

Cauldron

This is often portrayed in movies about witches as something used to make potions or boil children. While a cauldron can be used to make potions, it is most often used to hold water for scrying or to burn all your herbs for a spell. Most cauldrons are not giant pots because they don't need to be big. You are not going to be boiling goats or children, so you do not need a giant cauldron. The only time you would need a cauldron big enough to fit a human is if you were turning it into a Halloween-themed jacuzzi tub. The biggest cauldron you would need is no bigger than a quart, and even that is often more than enough room for what you require.

If you come across a spell that requires a giant cauldron, run in the other direction because the chances are that it is a dark magic spell and you do not want to dabble in dark magic at all. It can cost you your soul, and that is not something you want to gamble with.

Long Matches

Matches are an important thing to have in your ritual. You want long ones so that you can light a candle in a dish without worrying about burning yourself. You also want long matches because most of the time you should not move your candle from its position to light it; long fireplace matches give you the reach you need to light the candle without having to pick it up and move it.

You can use a barbecue lighter if you are not able to find fireplace matches, but a match is a more natural way to light the candle and does not emit any gas that will throw off the balance of your spell. You want a good balance when you do magic, so if you can get them, fireplace matches are the way to go. You can find them at your local supermarket.

Writing Utensil

Many spells require you to write something on a piece of paper and to do something with the paper. You can use either a pen or a pencil. They both work well, but if you are using a pen, it is best to use a fountain pen and an inkwell to be more traditional and really get the effect and energy you want from your spell. Be careful, though, because if you must write something down without lifting the writing utensil, you must make sure you have enough ink in the pen.

A pencil works well if you are going to be burning the paper immediately, or if you will not need it weeks down the road, as pencil fades quickly. However, for a spell in which you need to write your wish and then burn it or put it in a witch's jar, a pencil is the best way to go because it is wood and wood is natural. Even the graphite in the pencil is a composite of natural materials. If you haven't guessed by now, natural is the best way to go with magic because natural materials come from the earth and the use of them pleases the Great Mother, Gaea. Make sure that when you choose a pencil, you go with a number one or a number two, as anything over that contains too much graphite and cancels out the natural wood effect. Even though graphite is a composite of natural materials, it is a processed material, and too much of it can throw your spell out of balance.

Baskets

Baskets are used for a lot of reasons in the Wiccan religion. They carry supplies and hold pieces of the ritual. There are many styles of baskets you can use for different types of rituals. You must make sure you are using a basket that is the right size for the ritual you are performing. Baskets can be bought at the store if they are woven, but it is better if you make a basket yourself, weaving it out of natural materials.

To weave a basket, find materials of the same length (bark works the best); do a cross hatch weave for the basket and let it curl up on itself. Pull the weave tighter until it forms a bowl. You now have a basic basket. There are many basket tutorials you can find online.

You want to have a few different styles of baskets on hand for your rituals. They are not super important in the way of rituals, but some rituals call for them, and it is better to have them on hand than to find yourself short a basket.

Bucket of Water

A bucket of water is often used to cleanse your tools and your area before you perform your spell. It is always good to have a bucket of water on hand even if the spell does not call for it. You'll need one to clean any tool that falls on the ground so that it remains consecrated.

A bucket of water also keeps clean energy in your spell. You must make sure that your energy is clean, and when you use water, you help keep demons at bay. You can also make sure that your spell falls in the right hands of the right deity.

You want to make sure that you have a bucket of water and that you place it in your circle, not outside the circle. If you use the bucket of water correctly, it will significantly assist your spell. Let it assist your spell even if the spell does not call for it.

Ritual Wear

There are several things you should have on hand to wear for the rituals you will have to perform. You do not have to wear these for every spell, but you must have them on hand because when you are performing a true ritual, you should wear them as a sign of respect.

Rituals are performed most often on the solstices and at other times mentioned on the wheel of the year. These celebrations are very important in the Wiccan traditions; if you want to be part of the religion, it is best to make sure you observe them well. You do not want to ignore them, as they are part of a tradition. In the Wiccan religion, tradition is important, and you should try to keep it up. The beauty of Wicca is that you get to choose, but it can upset the deities if you approach this religion with a blasé attitude. You do not want to offend the deities if you want your spells to work because they are the ones that make the magic happen. You want them to want to help you, and you want them to answer your calls with eagerness. If you respect them and the traditions, they will respond to you with excitement to help.

Rituals are all different, and everyone performs his or her rituals a little differently. What ties them all together are the types of spells and the attire you wear while performing them. You want to wear the right attire because it shows that you respect the ritual and that you are willing to go the extra mile to show the deities that you mean business, that you are not just dabbling in magic for fun. This may seem like a good hobby, but it is a religion. Granted, it is a little bit more relaxed of a religion than you may be used to, but there are still expectations, and the more you follow them, the more the deities will recognize you and respect you. It is all about respect in the magical realm. You must respect the world; in return, the world will respect you.

Pentacle

This is an important part of the Wiccan religion. The pentacle is often confused with the pentagram when, in reality, they are two different things. The pentacle represents all that is pure and right in the world. It is surrounded by a circle and is upright. The five points represent the five elements, not the five layers of hell like the pentagram represents. The pentacle is often carved into magical tools to give them the proper energy so that the tools do not need to seek energy from undesirable entities. You should also have it carved into your altar. It is a good idea to use one to mark out your circle as well. The more you have, the more protected you are from demonic spirits trying to take over your magical spell and twist you into doing their bidding.

You can even wear the pentacle. You can get a pendant and have it on a necklace or a bracelet. In fact, both are great; a bracelet with several pentacle charms also helps. You can have it sewn into your robes or carved on your wand. There are so many options for wearing the pentacle that it is not funny. You can even have it printed on shoes. Of course, there is such a thing as overkill. If you have the pentacle printed on your shoes and sewn into your robe, you do not need jewelry covered in pentacles. You can save the jewelry for gemstones that will help the ritual spell of the night you are celebrating.

Gemstone Jewelry

There are several different gemstones you can wear during these rituals; which ones you choose depend on what you are trying to accomplish when you are performing the spell. The gemstones give the magic a boost because they can reflect energy as you are performing a spell. If you wear the right stones for the right ritual, you can release a powerful magic without using all the energy in your body. However, it is still a good idea to eat well and be well rested before any ritual because of the amount of energy it takes. You will probably be tired afterward, but that is okay because rituals can take a lot out of even a strong witch.

Gemstones will help reduce the amount of energy needed for a ritual so that you may need only a nap rather than to sleep for a full day and a half or more. Some people feel like they are going to go into a coma if they try to perform a ritual that is too complicated for their bodies. Avoid the comatose state; search for stones that are good for certain rituals and wear them shamelessly.

Jewelry with Sigils

Many Wiccans wear jewelry with sigils and wear them proudly. These are little symbols that represent the ritual you are going to perform. However, if you are already laden with jewelry, the sigils may be better left to robe decoration. You can hang them from the hem of your robe. Too much jewelry will counteract the productivity that the other types of jewelry bring to the spell.

Ritual Robes

A robe makes the ritual seem that much more official. I know what you are thinking when you think 'robe.' You are probably either thinking of the crushed velvet Merlin-style robe or the cushiony towel-like bathrobe. Neither is what you are looking for. You want a Wiccan-style robe. They are generally made of silk or satin and are dark purple or black. You want to have some ceremonial robes because they show that you are willing to respect the religion and make yourself look presentable when you are performing a ritual. They are also a lot less restricting than everyday clothes and allow you to move throughout your circle with ease. Of course, you should wear loose clothing underneath them, but the whole idea is to be free and able to move about with ease and grace.

Cloaks

Along with your robes, you should have a ritual cloak. Hooded cloaks are the best, in the case of inclement weather or if someone sees you in the woods performing a ritual, as you can hide your face. This world is not too kind to those who try to do magic. They equate all magic to Satan worship, which is very stereotypical and judgmental because only a very small percent of people who perform magic are devil worshipers.

Your cloak should match your robe; it is a good idea to have a pentacle sewn into it as well. A half-moon doesn't hurt either, as the half-moon is the symbol of Mother Goddess herself, and using this symbol will appeal to her greatly.

Ritual wear is very important. It is a good idea to have all these things on hand so that when you perform the ritual, you can appeal to the deities, that they may hear your spells throughout the year. You want them to want to help you, and this is one way to show them the respect they want to see.

Tools and Ingredients for Spell Work Parchment

This is an older, more natural style of paper, and it is getting harder and harder to find. Most of the time you must go to a Wiccan supply store or a stationary store if you can find one. Parchment is very important because when you are performing a spell that requires you to write something down, it is best to use parchment due to its being the most natural type of paper. Magic seems just to roll off this paper. Think about it, whenever you read a book that talks about magic, it has always been written on parchment using old-style pens. That is because the Wiccan traditions use the most natural things they can find. If you can make a quill out of a bird feather, that is the best pen there is. Parchment is just one of those things that makes the spell that much better because it is natural. You do not have to use it; it is just a little helper to boost the strength of the spell.

Candles

Candles are another important part of magic. They represent fire and can bring about magic themselves, depending on their color. If you are using candles, you should choose the style and shape based on what you want to do and if you want it to burn all the way down. Candles can serve many purposes in the magical world. They can be messengers to the spirit world when you burn a wish on a piece of paper. They can use their smoke to carry your magic to where it needs to go. They can represent one of the most volatile elements there is, and they can be used for light and warmth. Candles are a necessity in your witch's pantry. Make sure you have several kinds, styles, and colors. However, make sure they are not scented because the scent can mess with the magic.

Crystals, Incense, Herbs, and Other Spellbinders

Spellbinders are important, and pretty much every spell calls for at least one of them. Often, a spell will call for multiple spellbinders, which is a great thing because one is good, two are great, and three create a spell that can't be beaten. Any more than three is overkill, though, as they will begin to drown each other out, essentially making each one ineffective. You want effectiveness; otherwise, you will not have much luck with your spells. So, remember, more than three spellbinders is overkill.

Mortar and Pestle

This is an important thing to have because you want to be able to grind your herbs so that you make them into poultices and do other things with them. Every witch should have a few different sizes on hand and use them regularly.

Hand Drum or Music

Rhythmic music is a good thing to have when you are performing a ritual because it gives you a steady beat to follow when you move around the circle. The more rhythmic you are, the more grace you will show, and the more smoothly your magic will litigate itself upon the world. You want to use smooth movements when working a spell because you want your spell to go smoothly.

Empty Bottles and Jars

These are important because you will need them for various things, such as witch jars and making essential oils for your spells. You want to have several on hand so that you will have them when you need them. Garage sales are a good place to find them; just make sure you wash them out well.

Section 3

Finding and Purchasing Your Tools

Buying Online

The internet. Oh, what a wonderful invention it is. You can find anything you need online, and all it takes is a simple Google search. There are so many things you can find on the internet that it is insane. You can even find your tools and other things you will need for spells. However, you must be careful and always read the reviews before purchasing because sometimes you will not get what you think you are getting because companies can trick you with wording. Make sure you read the reviews and product description to find what you are looking for.

Purchasing in Person

If you live in an area that is more populated or more eccentric, you may be able to find a store that sells Wiccan tools. You can go there and see for yourself that you are getting what you need. Plus, you can talk to the person running the shop and get advice. Many shop owners have been in the religion for years and are eager to help newcomers find themselves. You do not get that with an online experience.

Consider the Items' Origins

This means considering how natural vs. how processed it is. You want to make sure that you are getting supplies as close to natural as you possibly can. If you can't get pure natural, find the purest form you possibly can. This is a lot easier to do when you buy in person because you can talk to the shop owner and get information about the product right from the source.

Unless you are rolling in cash, you are probably looking for ways to save. It is always best to go affordable when at all possible. Sometimes that means making an item yourself or buying it on sale if you cannot make it yourself. However, there are some things you should splurge on, such as a matching chalice and athame. These are things you use in a ritual, and that should show that you are serious about the religion. If you absolutely cannot afford it, try looking online for a second-hand set. The internet is great for this. It doesn't have to be expensive to look expensive.

More Wicca Books by Author

- *Empath: How to Flourish as an Empath & Little Known History of Empaths*
- *Third Eye: Proven Techniques to Increase Intuition and Psychic Awareness, Forgotten History of the Third Eye in the Ancient Americas*
- *Auras: Beginner's Guide and Tips & Tricks*
- *Psychic: How to Unlock Your Psychic Abilities and Enhance Intuition*
- *Astrology: Character, Essence, and the Nature of the 12 Zodiac Signs*

The link below leads to Valerie's Amazon author page where you can find other Wicca books and much more!

http://amzn.to/2dZA84h

CPSIA information can be obtained
at www.ICGtesting.com
Printed in the USA
BVHW071936030920
587909BV00001B/77